Discovering Dumfriesshire

Already published:
Discovering Aberdeenshire
Discovering Ayrshire
Discovering East Lothian
Discovering Fife
Discovering Galloway
Discovering Inverness-shire
Discovering Lewis and Harris
Discovering The Water of Leith
Discovering West Lothian

Forthcoming:
Discovering Argyll
Discovering Arran
Discovering Speyside
Discovering the Cotswolds

Discovering Dumfriesshire

ANDY MURRAY

JOHN DONALD PUBLISHERS LTD
EDINBURGH

DEDICATION:

To my wife Jacqui, who gave me all the encouragement I needed and put up with me against the odds.

ISBN 0 85976 294 7

Phototypesetting by Newtext Composition Ltd., Glasgow.
Printed in Great Britain by Bell & Bain Ltd., Glasgow.

Acknowledgements

A fair number of people helped in different ways during the preparation of this, my first, book. Several of them are people I have met, interviewed or shared a joke with during my eight years as a journalist in south-west Scotland (they are too numerous to list).

I am particularly indebted to Bill Laidlaw, of *Dumfriesshire Newspapers*, whose late father was rash enough to employ me in my first job as a reporter. Bill kindly allowed me to howk through several boxes of old photographs, some of which are used in the book. His assistance is greatly appreciated.

I thank Ian Rogers for producing sketches and maps for the odd whisky and lemonade, Noel Dinwiddie of Dumfries for always having some new titbit of local history with which to fascinate me, and Alistair Cowper and his helpful staff at the reference department of the Ewart Library in Dumfries for putting up with my, often unusual, requests. I also thank Bert Houston, rival freelance journalist from Dumfries, who provided me with the link between Dumfriesshire and Sherlock Holmes. Eileen Pringle and Helen Darke were also good enough to help me with source material.

In conclusion I want to thank the late Mr William McDowall, the historian of Dumfries who more than a century ago wrote a book which was to be incredibly handy during the last eight years of my life.

Contents

Introduction

Dumfriesshire, my home county, was gobbled up by Dumfries and Galloway region in 1975 and reconstituted as two districts named after its three main river valleys: Nithsdale and Annandale and Eskdale. Old habits die hard, however, and to most people in the eastern section of a region known deservedly as 'Scotland in Miniature', their postal address is still Dumfriesshire.

Old Dumfriesshire was bordered in the north-west by Ayrshire, in the south-west by Kirkcudbrightshire, in the east by Roxburghshire, Selkirkshire and Cumberland, and in the north by Lanarkshire and Peeblesshire. In the south and south-east it was washed by the shores of the Solway Firth, beloved of smugglers.

The old county stopped at the 'Brig'en' o' Dumfries', although the present district of Nithsdale stretches down through John Paul Jones country to the gateway of the 'Scottish Riviera'. For logistical reasons, I have chosen to terminate my book at the Brig'en'.

Its position as a bulwark against the English during the fierce border wars ensured Dumfriesshire a significant share of history, not all of which was honourable. The county recoiled at the raids of the Border Reivers, witnessed the oppression of the Covenanters, the wanton sacking of towns and the last witchcraft trial in Scotland. Sadly, too, it bowed its head in suffering after Britain's worst rail and air disasters.

In a lighter vein, Dumfriesshire was the home of Britain's first ostrich farmer, and of the first men in Scotland to plant turnips and rhubarb.

The tableau of famous characters associated with Dumfriesshire shows the names of Scott, Barrie, Hogg, MacDiarmid and Burns. And the county produced the inventor of the pedal cycle and that of the steamboat.

You could throw any number of clichés at Dumfriesshire and they would stick. It has fascinatingly diverse scenery, is plastered with ancient monuments, has Scotland's highest village, its second oldest library and its oldest post office. The county has ten square miles of lochs, and one of its lochs was, until recently, the world's sole habitat for a mystical freshwater fish. On the negative side, with Galloway, it is the most heavily afforested region of Britain.

Dumfriesshire also boasts Gretna Green, the international capital of romance, the so-called 'Marriage Mecca'. It has connections with Robert the Bruce, Bonnie Prince Charlie and Mary, Queen of Scots.

Dumfriesshire, with Nithsdale in the west, Annandale in the middle and Eskdale in the east, is essentially rural in character, although urbanisation is creeping up. The blood of its inhabitants has been mixed beyond recognition since the ancient times when the Selgovae (occupants of Dumfriesshire prior to the Romans) held sway; and the lowish price of houses has ensured a sizeable incursion of wealthy folk from the south of England, who will mix it even further.

The folk from Gretna are as different from those of Wanlockhead as the people of Langholm are dissimilar from those of Kirkconnel. Dumfriesshire is not uniform; it is absorbingly diverse.

To the prospective purchaser of a copy of this book, I would issue the following warning: it is neither a tourist guide nor a history book. It is something in between, a book about my native county's past, its present and its future – with the added ingredient of personal criticism. It is a highly selective, 'warts and all', opinionated work – the result of my belated discovery of the parts I spurned in my teens in favour of the bright lights. I have enjoyed discovering Dumfriesshire, and if a respectable number of people are moved to visit the forgotten south-west corner of Scotland on the strength of reading the following pages, then it will have been worth all the hard work.

SECTION 1: *ESKDALE*

CHAPTER 1
Gateway to Scotland

Gretna Green has generated more headlines than any other nook or cranny on the landmass of North Britain, although the hamlet is as much like the legendary Brigadoon as Hong Kong resembles Tristan da Cunha. Every summer's day the doors of some three dozen coaches are flung open to allow fresh batches of inquisitive tourists their first magical stroll on Caledonian soil. If they are after archetypal Scottish scenery they will have to hoof it further north to the hills and glens, but if they are happy with the Gretna Green experience and are in the market for trinkets and postcards for the converted biscuit-tin, then they have come to the right place.

Nevertheless, the village has attracted its share of VIPs. George V, for example, made the pilgrimage, as did Queen Mary, Prince Henry of Russia and David Lloyd George. An Arabian sultan and a Japanese viscount have also stayed. Charles Dickens, King Hussein of Jordan, the film stars Anthony Newley and Janette Scott, and the comedians Billy Connolly, Ken Dodd and Harry Secombe have also visited. Ian Botham has called in, too.

The Gretna Green phenomenon began in the year 1754 when the legal age for marrying without parental consent became twenty-one in England, but sixteen in Scotland. Elopements to the village became as fashionable as designer shirts and jeans are today: long before the A74 took traffic away from the old road through Longtown and Springfield, European aristocrats headed over the border with their sweethearts and coltish vigour to tie the matrimonial knot. They included the Marquis of Hastings, the Earl of Dundonald, Lord Erskine, the son of the King of Sicily and Duke Sforza of Rome.

A diarist wrote in 1780 (the year after the huntsman John Peel took the plunge at Gretna Green) that couples could be 'instantly united by a fisherman, a joiner or a blacksmith, who

Billy Connolly, 'the Big Yin', at the marriage mecca *(Courtesy: Dumfriesshire Newspaper Group)*

marry from two guineas a job to a dram of whisky'. Weddings were later conducted at Springfield, which was built in 1791, and at the Headless Cross. The toll bar, which was the first house in Scotland, also became a magnet for the betrothed, as did The Famous Old Blacksmith's Shop. David Linton made Gretna Hall one of the finest posting establishments between Edinburgh and London – and an attractive wedding venue for the well-to-do.

Eventually every tippling-house had its rival 'priest' who jabbered over a sermon of the Church of England and handed out marriage lines. When Richard Ayton, the travel writer, passed through in 1815, the marrying trade was in the hands of 'hedgers and ditchers', and he declared: 'At the risk of inciting the scorn of all masters and mistresses under twenty-

Joseph Paisley *(Courtesy: Adair Houston)*

one, I venture to raise my voice against this prophanation of a solemn and beautiful service by these vulgar mercenaries.' Gretna Green then consisted of three or four miserable huts, one of which acted as the post office and served whisky and oatcakes.

Ayton was not the only person to be perturbed by the mercenaries: to *bona fide* clergymen they were anathema. The Revd John Morgan, parish minister in the 1790s, was particularly scathing. He criticised the nobility for 'allowing their pockets to be picked by such miscreants'.

Morgan, whose salary must have been minuscule compared to the takings of your average Gretna Green priest, condemned them as 'impostors and priests of their own erection who have no right whatever either to marry or to exercise any part of the clerical function'.

The first of the impostors was Joseph Paisley, an erstwhile tobacconist and smuggler, who took up the marrying trade almost as soon as the ink had dried on the 1754 Marriage Act – and plied it for fifty-eight years. Paisley weighed in at twenty-five stones, and his favourite party trick was to bend a thick poker or straighten a horseshoe. It was his enormous power that created the Gretna Green blacksmith myth. According to Morgan, he was 'a fellow without literature, without morals and without manners whose irregular conduct has rendered him an object of detestation to all the sober and virtuous part of this neighbourhood'. But Paisley married many people of noble birth, and averaged sixty weddings a year, which netted him a cool £945 *per annum.* He got his couples mixed up once and united the wrong groom to the wrong wife. His reported reaction was: 'Aweel, jeest sort yersel's'.

Morgan reckoned that Paisley often gave out bogus marriage certificates when he was intoxicated. The witnesses were fictitious ones.

More anecdotes about Paisley would have been worth listening to, but the handicapped daughter of his successor, Robert Elliot, accidentally burned all the registers and documents. There is, however, existing evidence of one of the famous Gretna Green marriages, that of Sarah Child, the daughter of a London banker, to Lord Westmorland. Sarah's father, Robert, hired henchmen to drive north in pursuit of the elopers. And the posse did everything they could to stop the wedding. They even shot one of the horses pulling the couple's coach to Gretna Green. But Westmorland's servant saved the day by slipping behind Child's carriage and cutting the leather which held the frame to the springs. The result was that Robert Child lost both his daughter and his coach, but Sarah became Lady Westmorland as intended.

Charles Dickens stayed at Gretna Hall in 1852 and wrote in *Household Words* about the graffiti on the walls: 'John Anderson made a fool of himself at Gretna, 1831' was one example from an early Kilroy. Apparently Dickens was copying the hotel menu and an old man kept hovering around him. He expressed his annoyance whereupon the old codger told the novelist he could get him a cuddy-ride across the border for twopence.

Richard Rennieson, the last of the Gretna Green 'priests' *(Courtesy: Adair Houston)*

Weddings at Gretna Green became fewer after 1856 when Lord Brougham rushed a bill through Parliament making it necessary for one of the marriage partners to stay in Scotland for twenty-one days before the wedding. Ironically, Brougham had been married at Gretna Green.

However, the twentieth century has seen a steady flow of couples to the village. Many of them met Richard Rennieson, the teetotaller and former rabbit catcher, who officiated at The Famous Old Blacksmith's Shop from 1927 until 1940. He wed 5147 couples over the anvil; an old guidebook said of him: 'His vitality as priest and showman is remarkable. He is as well known as any celebrity in the land.' Rennieson married an MP, a Secretary of State's daughter and the son of a former Moderator of the General Assembly of the Church of Scotland. Another of his grooms was a Dutchman who, reputedly, stood at nine feet three inches in his stocking soles. Rennieson finally hung up his hammer during the year of the Battle of Britain, and legal weddings over the anvil were outlawed the same year during the brief tenure of his successor, Robert McKennon.

Sir Ken Potter getting married to his bike at Gretna Green *(Courtesy: Dumfriesshire Newspaper Group)*

The priests are no more: all that remains is the mystique which attracts hundreds of thousands of people to Gretna Green from all over the world. Gretna Hall, now owned by North British Hotels, has a small museum of curios, including a 'mantrap'. The Famous Old Blacksmith's Shop has a display of paintings with a wedding theme. There are also some intriguing letters and telegrams received by Rennieson, one of which reads: 'Marriage ceremony must not be performed. Bridegroom known ex-convict. Girl's mother in state of collapse.'

Mock marriages are ultra-popular nowadays, and many foreigners and expatriates are 'wed' over the anvil. The ceremony is not legally binding unless it is done by a clergyman, but some couples take some persuading that they are not really married. No holds have been barred for practical jokers, either. I remember seeing one Sir Ken Potter being married to his bike, and in the late 1970s the Barbarians rugby team paid a clandestine visit, in order to avoid attracting anti-apartheid demonstrators, to Gretna Green. The South Africans witnessed an anvil wedding before being bussed to the Borders to prepare for matches against Hawick and Galashiels.

Local businessmen go to bed happy at night, but as kilted guides blow the bagpipes and spin the tales at Gretna Green, serious aspiring brides and grooms-to-be head down the road to a side street in Gretna township where registrar Pat Bryden, MBE, has united over 9000 couples since 1955. She has married people from all over the world: Chinese, Africans, Russians, Israelis and Australians. St Valentine's Day, and 29 February during Leap Years are busy periods.

Pat Bryden has seen her share of melodrama and comedy, too. She married her great-niece, and did the honours for a bride dressed up as Donald Duck and a groom in a crash helmet. During one ceremony a Spanish father burst in and threatened his son with a knife; at another a policeman rushed in to prevent a man committing bigamy. And a Russian once travelled several thousand miles to ask Miss Bryden to divorce his daughter, seeing as she had married her in the first instance.

In 1984, all the national newspapers 'splashed' on a story about a schoolmaster who had run away with a sixteen-year-old pupil to get married at Gretna, and the elopement rekindled interest in Gretna weddings. Records are now broken every year as droves of young and old couples prove that the age of romance is alive and well.

As I write, the 'Marriage Mecca' is being earmarked for a multi-million pound 'Gateway to Scotland' centre by two rival property developers. The race to turn Gretna and Gretna Green into Scotland's number one tourist hotspot began when a company of leisure consultants produced a blueprint for the Scottish Development Agency, the Scottish Tourist Board and the five local councils. They recommended more than cashing in on the wedding theme: they planned to haul Robert Burns on board along with Rob Roy, Robert the Bruce, Bonnie Prince Charlie and the Loch Ness Monster. They saw scope for fire-eaters, jugglers, Punch and Judy shows and a 'ghost-train style of experience' reflecting the tales of the Border Reivers and Gretna Green's rise to fame. They wanted flags draped across the metal bridge over the border – a bridge which many people want demolished on the grounds that it is an eyesore. Mock

Scottish passports and all sorts of allied mawkish hokum were also in the pipeline.

Counter-proposals came in thick and fast; Adair Houston, whose family have owned The Famous Old Blacksmith's Shop for over a century, condemned Dumfries and Galloway Regional Council for proposing to use state money to back the complex on a 'bogus location with no historical authenticity' at Gretna rather than at Gretna Green.

It all led to a rift between Gretna and Gretna Green, the latter thinking that the former would benefit from the heritage and romance associated with the latter. Adair Houston put his money where his mouth was, and started building a tourist information office at Gretna Green. He has also vowed to build his own complex – whether or not the council-backed proposals get going. He plans an Agridome for livestock exhibitions, a landscaped country park, a heritage centre and a pipe band area. The Houstons rightly boast that they have raised the profile of Gretna Green immeasurably over the years: nearly every northbound coach operator calls in at the family's Famous Old Blacksmith's Shop, which has had publicity in such varied publications as the *Los Angeles Times* and the German edition of *Playboy*. There have also been slots on Bavarian, Belgian and Japanese television.

An even more interesting proposal was put forward in spring, 1989, by Decorative Stained Glass, an Annan-based company. Their plan was for a Scottish Crafts Centre at the border: a huge 'Multiplex' entertainment bowl and a King Arthur theme park. Director Drew Landsborough told the regional council that his 1000-seater complex would overlook the Solway Firth and lead Scotland with confidence into 1992 and the European jamboree. He envisaged statues of King Arthur, Sir William Wallace and Robert the Bruce, and four mini-video cinemas reflecting Scottish history and wildlife. In his submission, Mr Landsborough said: 'Madame Tussaud's might come in on a joint venture. Perhaps spectators could be wafted along from scene to scene in a flat-bottomed boat along a gently moving staircase – as at Disneyland.'

Why King Arthur, I hear you asking! Well, Mr Landsborough is convinced of the theory that the kingdom of the mystical king was between Dumfries and Gretna, and the

'Border City' of Carlisle was his Camelot. Mr Landsborough's glass dome, accordingly, would have been topped by 'a gigantic King Arthur's crown': a walkway around the dome would have allowed visitors to the area to enjoy panoramic views of the Lakeland peaks across the water. To cap it all, there was to be a rose garden, showers, jacuzzis and a swimming pool with a tropical temperature where businessmen could unwind *en route* from Glasgow to London.

At the time of writing, two property companies (one in Stirling and one in London) have been shortlisted to go ahead with their proposals. Adair Houston is to build his rival complex a mile away. And Drew Landsborough's plans are not being ruled out. It all reminds me of Joseph Paisley's immortal words: 'Aweel, jeest sort yersel's!'

CHAPTER 2

A Community Under the Influence

When Joseph Paisley was performing his poker-twisting strong-arm antics and staggering through the village, the border township of Gretna was non-existent: there was only the parish of Graitney.

Gretna itself had to wait for the First World War to be born as a base for thousands of workers in the British Empire's biggest arsenal. Moorside was the coded name Sir Arthur Conan Doyle gave it when he was employed as a war propagandist. The creator of Sherlock Holmes described the place as 'one of the miracles of present-day Britain and perhaps the most remarkable place in the world'.

In true newsreel style, Conan Doyle wrote in *The Times* of 29 November 1916: 'Only a little more than a year ago, it was a lonely peat bog fringing the sea, with a hinterland of desolate plain, over which the gulls swooped and screamed. Then the great hand of the minister of munitions was stretched out to this inhospitable waste, for it chanced to lie with good rail and water connections, and not too remote from the centres of coal and iron.'

It was like a great development from the Wild West. Twenty-five thousand folk were building it and servicing it, and shiploads of workers were being drafted in from Ireland. Conan Doyle reckoned that when they were fully operational, the huge marshalling yards would have work for 12 000 men and women.

Redbrick houses went up for factory officials, and married navvies were consigned to 600 wooden huts built in rows from the Annan Road to the Solway. There were main offices, telephone stations, a staff club, a hospital, a cinema theatre and a row of shops.

The Solway coastline took on an ugly appearance from which it has never recovered. One writer walked the sixteen miles of military buildings from Mossband in England to Eastriggs in Scotland in 1920 and observed: 'It was as grievous a site as the blazes of the different works had been when seen from the distant hills during the time of service.'

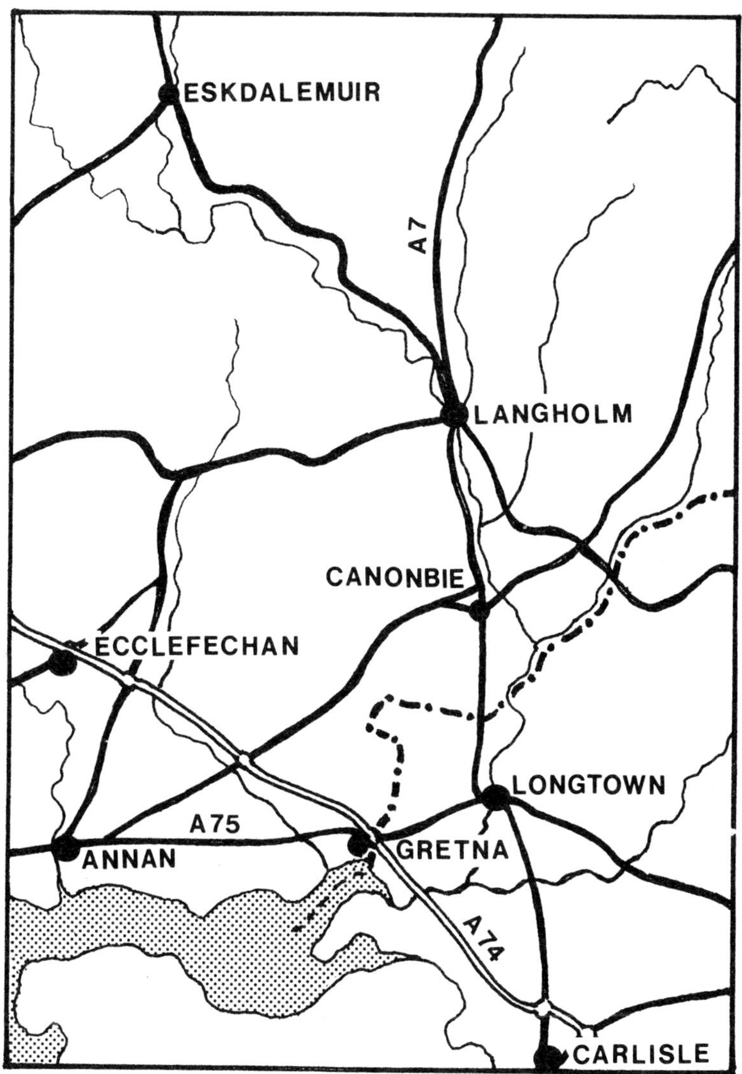

Map drawn by Ian A Rogers

The massive influx of alcohol-abusing labourers led to a change in the licensing laws: the introduction of a mini-nationalisation programme which lasted not only until the bullets stopped flying but for fifty-five years. The Prime

Minister David Lloyd George exclaimed: 'Drunkenness among munitions workers is doing more damage to the war effort than all the German submarines put together.'

Marauding navvies swooped down on Carlisle on pay night with their big wage packets, to get drunk, prompting one contemporary report that: 'The spectacle of stupefied men often turned violent by their nightly excesses can only offend the ordinary decent folk of this unfortunate town. But the spectacle of healthy young women rendered senseless by their manifest depravity can only be described as obscene. On a Saturday night this ancient town reminds us of those godless and debauched citadels in the Old Testament: those on which the Lord reeked terrible vengeance.'

The only train from Gretna to Carlisle arrived five minutes before closing-time, so the workers had a collection for the engine-driver each night to bribe him to arrive at the station a few minutes faster. The landlord of Boustead's Bar in Carlisle was another willing accomplice: he had a few hundred whiskies ready-poured for the thirsty and expectant navvies. Never in the field of human boozing has so much been consumed by so few – and in such a short time. The Edinburgh *Evening News* reported that there could be few places in the whole of Scotland where the war had brought about deeper social changes than 'the tract of land lying on the shore of the Solway Firth'.

When the State Management Scheme was introduced, the number of court appearances for drunkenness in Annan and Gretna decreased as dramatically as the production of munitions had gone downhill previously. Around the same time a State Management Scheme for pubs was introduced in the Cromarty Firth area owing to an outbreak of drunkenness at a submarine base in Dingwall. This was the only similar scheme in Britain.

During the Great War, Gretna was also the scene of what is still Britain's worst rail disaster. Human error marked 22 May 1915 down as a day of disaster. Two hundred and twenty passengers were killed and 246 injured when three trains collided at Quintinshill. The side-loops at the signal-box had been occupied by a goods train and an empty train, therefore the signalman put a slow train on the other main line until an express had passed. Incredibly, he forgot about the slow train and signalled a troop train through. It smashed into the stationary local train, and both lines were blocked by the debris. Seconds later the express from Carlisle ploughed into the wreckage.

Many people were burned to death by exploding cylinders of gas used for lighting. The fire raged for twenty-four hours and the two trains on the loop line were also gutted.

'It may be questioned whether in the long and bloodstained story of the debatable land where the tragedy took place, there is set down anything more startlingly and poignantly tragic than the fate which, in the course of a few minutes of shock and flame, practically wiped out of existence a half battalion of the 7th of Leith Royal Scots,' wrote *The Scotsman*. 'Of nearly 500 officers and men who were on their way from their homes to fight their country's battle at the front, little more than fifty answered the roll-call – an incident as heart-rendingly mournful as any recorded in Border history.'

One journalist, moreover, wrote that, even to a Britain punch-drunk on the casualty figures from the Flanders trenches, it was a disaster that defied description and defeated the headline-writers.

Investigators concluded that the force of the collision had reduced the length of the troop train from 213 to sixty-seven yards. An eye-witness described the concertina-like white-hot steel wagon-frames 'twisting and curling like dying leaves'. Doctors risked death to amputate limbs in a bid to save men trapped under carriages. Another observer stated, somewhat grotesquely, that bodies without arms, legs and heads, had protruded from every part of the troop train.

It had been a dark day for Gretna, but an even more sorrowful one for Leith, from where many of the soldiers came. One of the rescuers at the scene was Alexander Sutherland Neill, who was eventually to found the revolutionary Summerhill schools but was then stand-in dominie at Gretna Public School. Neill got to Quintinshill by bicycle, after the postman had rushed through the village to tell them a Zeppelin had bombed the troop train.

Neill was later to write in his memoirs: 'The scene resembled a silent film. The only sounds were the hissing of the engines

Chaos at Quintinshill watched by two cyclists *(Courtesy: British Rail).*

and the pops of the cartridges as fire crept along the wreckage. Men were lying dead or dying; one soldier with both legs torn off asked me for a cigarette, and he grinned as I lit it up for him. "May as well lose them here as in France," he said lightly. He died before the cigarette was half smoked.'

Dying men called out for their mothers: it was all like a horror movie, and Neill reckoned that officers shot some of the men hopelessly pinned under the carriages.

What really happened at Quintinshill is still a state secret lodged in the Scottish Record Office in a file which will not be released until the year 2015. What is known is that the legal position was complicated because the accident had occurred just on the border and twenty-seven of the victims had died on English soil. The two guilty signalmen, James Tinsley and George Meakin, were tried at the High Court in Edinburgh and found guilty. Meakin went down for eighteen months; Tinsley was sentenced to three years' penal servitude, but suffered a nervous breakdown while in jail. He would later have plenty of time to reflect on his mistakes, for he died, an old and broken man, in 1967.

When the First World War finished Gretna became a fairly depressed area: while its neighbour Gretna Green had depended on marital affairs, Gretna had relied on martial affairs. Come the next war, the township came into its own again, and military stores were established in the area, making it a sitting target to resourceful enemies. The community was shattered on 7 April 1941, when a Nazi bomb missed the munitions works and landed on the Masonic Hall. Some of the district's leading Freemasons were wiped out, including some prominent Dumfries businessmen down for a lodge meeting. Wartime censorship allowed only short reports in the local newspapers (headed 'passed by the censor'). Thinking the public did not have sufficient brain cells to add two and two together, the papers printed obituaries of several people who died at Gretna that night, but didn't give the cause of death.

One of them was the Revd John Stafford, a county councillor and Grand Superintendent of the Royal Arch Masonry in Dumfriesshire. During the First World War, Stafford had been on the Gretna School committee, and had been one of the objectors to the liberal educational methods used by Neill. In his book, *A Dominie's Log,* Neill wrote that Stafford rode around on a strange multi-coloured bicycle with a hammock for a saddle, the eternal fag dangling from his lips. He preached on the evils of drink on a Sunday, yet was not averse to a dram or two himself. Stafford also, apparently, sacked his odd-job man for teaching the family parrot to swear, although the best dirty stories in the area were reputed to come from the minister.

Stafford clashed with Neill because the dominie wanted to abolish the three 'Rs and homework. Also intent on scrapping corporal punishment Neill threw the tawse into the school stove when it was freezing, and he closed the school once when it was too cold to teach, despite the fact that the Board chairman had refused him permission to do so.

Neill was branded as an eccentric rather than a dangerous revolutionary, although he preached against war and declared that a pacifist had much more moral courage than three army corps. In between times he helped the children build snowmen in winter and instructed them to write autobiographies of a hat, a chair or an old penny – or a conversation between a shed and a pond.

Not far from Gretna Public School stands Gretna Old Church, which was burned down in 1736 when the thatched

Gretna Old Parish Church *(Photograph: J Donabie, Gretna)*

roof was set alight by men shooting swallows. Nine years later, Bonnie Prince Charlie's southbound troops threw stones at the manse door and stole a beehive. On their retreat from Derby 144 Highlanders were remanded in custody in the church pending trial in Carlisle, and the congregation attended an *ex tempore* service on the village green. Bonnie Prince Charlie's Cottage can be visited in Gretna Green to this day.

Still on kirks: there was one called Redkirk on a narrow point of land on the Solway coast at Gretna, but it was washed away by a strong tide. The Revd James Roddick wrote, rather inelegantly, for the *New Statistical Account of Dumfriesshire* in 1834: 'Some old people yet remember the unwelcome sight of bones and coffins protruding from the banks, or collected from the beach into a trough which had been used as a font in the days of popery.'

Nearby – in fact, ironically on the present site of the CAD Longtown ammunition depot – Scotland suffered its worst military debacle. The battle of Solway Moss is supposed to have led to the premature death of James V and thus altered the course of history. As many as 12 000 Scots were taken prisoner, and only one Englishman. The king is thought to have wept as he watched the battle from Burnswark (an extinct volcano near Ecclefechan).

Many Scots drowned in the moss while escaping, only to be accidentally disentombed many centuries later, according to William McDowall in his *History of Dumfries*. He may have been referring to the events of 17 December 1771, when the Solway Moss burst and spread. Thirty families were made homeless and 200 acres of good farmland were flooded with a quagmire of peat. A subsequent downpour flooded another 300 acres.

Epilogue: 1988

Preparations were under way to mark the 450th anniversary of the battle. While Europe is basking in the single European market, the Auld Enemies (represented by the English Kirkandrews-on-Esk and Arthuret parish councils, and by Gretna and Rigg Community Council on the Scottish side) will symbolically be burying the hatchet. It was being organised by Mike Scott, an Englishman, and chairman of the Scottish council.

CHAPTER 3

The Debatable Land

A 'walloper' of a stone the size of a man and more stands in a field next to the Solway shore outside Gretna, bearing no sign that it used to be as important a place as the Great Wall of China or Checkpoint Charlie. The Lochmabenstane, a unique landmark deposited by a huge iceberg or hauled from afar with enormous manpower to act as a Druidical temple or mark the burial place of the seventh century warrior, Maponus, is a monument to the days when a no man's land existed between Scotland and England – as volatile as those which have in more recent times partitioned the northern and southern portions of Vietnam and Korea.

An area ten miles long and three miles wide between the rivers Sark and Esk was claimed for centuries by both Scotland and England. Neither country, however, could govern it, not least because its inhabitants were hit-men, operators of protection rackets or folk heroes and commandos – depending upon which side you were on. They were the Border Reivers, whose exploits filled local ballads and exasperated kings and nobles. As the great Elizabethan antiquarian Camden put it in 1586, they were 'a warlike kind of men who have been infamous for Robberies and Depradations'. Although Sir Walter Scott and other romanticists wrote stirringly of the Borderers, they lived for personal gain rather than out of patriotism.

Robert Louis Stevenson wrote later of the Border Scots and English: 'Here are two people almost identical in blood – the same in language and religion; and yet a few years of quarrelsome isolation – in comparison with the great historical cycles – have so separated their thoughts and ways, that not unions nor mutual dangers, not steamers nor railways, nor all the king's horses nor all the king's men seem able to obliterate the broad distinction.' But the truth is that Scot pillaged Scot, and Englishman pillaged Englishman; and there were members of the Grahams, Elliots, Armstrongs or Nixons on both sides of the great divide, who fought one another. Reivers

A young-looking Bryan Armstrong (a former colleague of the author) stands by the famous Lochmabenstane near Gretna *(Courtesy: Dumfriesshire Newspaper Group)*

reived north and south as well as sideways, backwards and forwards.

The debatable land had belonged to Scotland up until the fourteenth century, but from then until the Union of the Crowns the subjects of both Scotland and England grazed their herds on its bleak, poor pastureland by day and removed them before sunset – lest they were appropriated by Clym of the Cleugh, Hobbie Noble, Jock o' the Side, or ruthless desperadoes from the other big families.

The Armstrongs were reivers who stamped their name upon the Border ballads more than any of the other warring tribes who jostled to press their authority on the debatable land: they were the most dreaded clan on the frontier. Johnnie Armstrong, for example, was a man who could command the power of 3000 comrades. To many, he was a Robin Hood type; to others he was a cruel tyrant chieftain. To James V he was a menace who had to be got rid of. And he did. According to the ballad, the king summoned Johnnie from the Armstrong stronghold of Hollows near Canonbie, promising a pardon. Johnnie, alias Blak Jok, and fifty horsemen rode to Carlanrig near Hawick to meet the king, who proceeded to sentence them to death.

James is reputed to have said: 'What wants yon knave that a king should have?' Johnnie offered to bring him any Englishman, from a duke downwards, dead or alive on any stated day. He also offered forty cavalrymen, twenty-four milk-white horses, the produce of two dozen mills, as much English gold as four men could carry and a rent on every property between Hawick and Newcastle.

King James was unimpressed. Johnnie and his mobsters were sent to meet their maker on oak trees. Armstrong's final defiant declaration before he was hanged was: 'To seik het water beneath cauld ice, surely it is a great follie – I hae asked grace at a graceless face, but there is nane for my men and me.'

Local tradition has it that the oak trees where the reivers were launched into eternity never grew leaves again, but one writer wrote that the English were as glad of Johnnie's execution as America would have been at the death of Al Capone.

Another notable Armstrong was Archie, a dexterous sheep-rustler who left Eskdale when it became too hot for him. Records show that he was appointed court jester to James VI, a post which he held for several years. His Border temper was his undoing: he was fired for falling out with Archbishop Laud and others, whereupon he disappeared from history.

The Armstrongs had also sired Kinmont Willie, who was probably the best known of the Border Reivers. His command of some of the most desperate rustlers of the sixteenth century earned him a niche in Borders history. He took much booty on both sides of the unsettled borderline – so much that James VI swooped down on Dumfriesshire in 1587 to capture him. But he holed himself up on Tarras Moss, as inaccessible a place as was possible (and one which the poet Hugh MacDiarmid would later refer to as 'a Bolshevik bog').

When Willie was sixty-five years old he carried out his most daring raid – leading 1000 men into Tynedale for thousands of cattle and sheep and £300 in spoils.

Willie was apprehended by skullduggery: the Warden of the English West March used a sacrosanct day of truce in March 1596 to capture him at Kershopefoot. He should have been safe for twenty-four hours from sunrise to sunrise, but convention was brushed aside. The warden, Lord Scrope, took him to Carlisle Castle, 'pinioned like a common malefactor, arms tied behind him, legs bound under his horse's belly', thereby breaking a code which was as sacred as the Corsicans' law of silence.

Kinmont Willie was freed in accordance with a plan hatched on Langholm racecourse. It was an SAS-style manoeuvre led by Sir Walter Scott of Buccleuch, the Keeper of Liddesdale.

Willie's sorties had gone on despite the establishment of a new border after the Treaty of Norham in 1552. It followed the Kershope burn from Scotch Knowe to the Liddel, then along the Liddel to the Esk near Canonbie and down the Esk again to the beginning of the Scots Dyke.

The dyke was a ditch four miles long which settled for ever the land which had been debated for centuries. It was the first artificial border in Europe, but it is now woefully neglected and buried beneath mosses and lichens – a universe away from the fierce anarchic no man's land of history. That debatable land is now a characterless jungle of pylons and scrubland, punctuated by the occasional appealing clump of birch where reed buntings and treecreepers nest – safe from cut-throats.

And the Lochmabenstane, where did it figure in Border history? Armies met at the stone. It was on the invasion route between Burgh-by-Sands and the Scottish ford of Sulwath; and it was the mustering ground for the royal levies of Dumfriesshire and Galloway. Criminals were tried there, and days of truce observed there. It was a ransom point and the venue of summit meetings. As one historian put it: 'The Lochmabenstane was a landmark of extraordinary interest, past which, in alternate flux and reflux, like the sea beside it, there swept for centuries successive invasions.'

In 1296, the stone saw the advance of the first battalion in the war of independence; in 1449 it saw the battle of the Sark, and in later years it is regularly cited in *Pitcairn's Criminal Trials*. Many Border Reivers got their come-uppance at the Lochmabenstane.

Present day Border Reivers, Langholm *(Photograph: Norman Allan, Langholm)*

The Union of the Crowns closed an exciting chapter in Border history – or a bloody one depending upon whether you liken the Reivers to Robin Hood and his Merry Men or to Stalinist terrorists. After Queen Elizabeth I died, the Grahams, the Armstrongs, the Elliots and others made a last heist on English soil: they got as far as Penrith and returned north with 1280 cattle and 3807 sheep and goats.

James VI abolished the warden system and began to 'pacify' the Borderland (pacification being a more official form of terrorism). Strongholds were razed to the ground. Many crooks were hanged; other outlaws were rounded up and packed off to the army to fight in Bohemia and Ireland. Armstrongs were used in the plantations of Protestants in Ulster. Flitting became obligatory too, for the Grahams, who went to Spain and Holland. They returned to Eskdale but were banished to the boglands of Roscommon and Connaught 'where a change of air will make in them a change in manners'.

But the Border reiving spirit remains in the brigands' countless ancestors. Rugby, the area's proud regiments,

Cumberland wrestling and the notorious dourness of the Border Scot are the legacies.

According to George MacDonald Fraser, the author of *The Steel Bonnets,* former US President Richard Nixon was the perfect example of a Border Scot: 'The blunt heavy features, the dark complexion, the burly body, and the whole air of dour hardness are as typical of the Anglo-Saxon frontier as the Roman Wall. Take thirty years off his age and you could put him straight into the front row of the Hawick scrum and hope to keep out of his way. It is difficult to think of any face that would fit better under a steel bonnet.'

CHAPTER 4

The Muckle Toon

The late and lamented Eddie Armstrong MBE, who died while I was researching this book, used to employ the catchphrase 'out of the world and into Langholm'. So great was his love for the grey border home town he served so well.

Eddie, who was town clerk of 'the Muckle Toon' from the Second World War until he retired to oppose successfully his former Provost Jimmy Grieve in the new-fangled regional council elections, earned the honorary title, Mr Langholm.

The mill town fiercely embraces traditions such as the annual Common Riding and rugby. Langholm (pronounced Lang-oom) has the oldest rugby side in the Borders, and the folk are proud to relate that it all began in 1871 when the men took up the sport as an alternative to curling, owing to a succession of mild winters. The town can also boast of possessing Scotland's oldest town band, which first marched through the streets with the Royal Scots Greys after the battle of Waterloo.

The Common Riding dates back to 1759, although it is held on the anniversary of a far more ancient festival known as the 'Langholm summer fair', one of Scotland's greatest lamb sales. The boundaries were then patrolled on foot by the town drummer, but after 1816 horses became the order (some would say the *ordure*) of the day. Nowadays on the last Friday of every July up to 200 riders follow the Cornet up the Kirk Wynd to the common land in the surrounding hills. Langholmites from all over the country try to get back for the Common Riding: it has something of a religious ring about it that is scarcely credited by outsiders. In the days when trains ran, on the eve of the Common Riding, the town band used to meet the returning exiles and escort them through the town. It was a sentimental affair.

Just as Gretna people have more in common with the people of Carlisle than with those in Dumfries, Langholm's heart lies in the east. And the folk have from time to time sought annexation to Roxburghshire: the ultimate remedy to being treated as an outpost by councils in the west.

Annual festivities in the Muckle Toon of Langholm *(Photograph: Norman Allan, Langholm)*

Langholm is, indeed, an isolated community: it even has its own newspaper, the oldest penny newspaper in Scotland. Although it is the 'Gateway to the Scottish Borders', its detachment from the mainstream of tourism is compounded by a lack of signposting, which is quite reprehensible for a town which is the only sizeable one on the A7 between Longtown and Hawick.

The potential for tourism in Eskdale is great. Hugh MacDiarmid was born in Langholm. Thomas Telford first saw the light of day in nearby Westerkirk. Henry Scott Riddell, the author of Scotland's *Marseillaise*, 'Scotland Yet', was born at Sorbie in the Ewes Valley a few miles north of Langholm. Another famous Langholmite, William Julius Mickle, is commemorated by a plaque outside the town hall. He translated the Portuguese epic, the Lusiad of Camoens and wrote the popular song, 'There's nae luck aboot the hoose'.

In purely scenic terms the area surrounding Langholm is excellent. The Wauchope Valley inspired Wordsworth to verse, and Eskdale prompted MacDiarmid's friend, Thomas Cairncross, to write:

Typical Eskdale scenery

It lies by the heather slopes,
Where God spilt the wine of the moorland,
Brimming the beaker of hills. Lone it lies:
A rude outpost: challenging stars and dawn,
And down from remoteness
And the Balladland of the Forest

The Pictish Esk trails glory,
Rippling the quiet eaves
With the gold of the sun.

In 1988, the authorities were beginning to wake up to the missed opportunities in Langholm and Eskdale, and the local tourist board produced a development study. There were proposals for a woollen heritage trail, a Thomas Telford Centre and an events strategy to commemorate the Border Reivers. Regrettably, however, the study made only passing reference to Hugh MacDiarmid. It was a familiar transgression: ten years after the poet's death, there were no signposts to the bronze memorial to him on a hillside outside town. Langholm's most famous son, the much-written about leader of the Scottish renaissance and one of the greatest geniuses of the twentieth century, is forgotten by most of his fellow Langholmites. They tend not to advertise his memorial (the work of outlanders) which is a great pity. The regional council's roads department has consistently opposed signposting for the MacDiarmid Memorial on the grounds that the access road from the A7 is hazardous, and there are no adequate parking facilities there.

Local indifference to MacDiarmid, however, is nothing new. He was not even given a mention by the minister in the *Third Statistical Account of Dumfriesshire* although he had the world at his feet before its publication in 1962. He had already been awarded an honorary degree by Edinburgh University, and in the citation his name had been ranked alongside those of Thomas Carlyle and David Hume. The Revd JL Cotter, however, chose to ignore MacDiarmid.

MacDiarmid, born Christopher Murray Grieve the son of the Langholm postman, had of course blotted his copy-book by lampooning the townsfolk in his early work, but he made up for it in many ways with his verses about the hills, glens and burns.

His love for Eskdale shines through, for example in the following verses:

And a' the rivers, the Esk, the Ewes,
The Wauchope, the Nith, I dooked in and fished
Guddled and girned – the hert o' a loon
Nae better playgr'und could ever ha'e wished.

Hugh MacDiarmid's widow, Valda Grieve, with Jake Harvey, who sculpted the bronze memorial to him, near Langholm. Valda died in May, 1989. *(Courtesy: The Scotsman Publications Ltd)*

And the wuds o' the Langfall and Kernigal
Whaur we picked the hines and got oor conkers
And dung the squirrels oot o' the trees
In the happy days when we were younkers.

One of the greatest insults to MacDiarmid was a report, in a Sunday newspaper in 1963, which speculated that he would be granted the Freedom of Langholm. The then Provost Jimmy Grieve, who died in 1988, was quoted as saying that the conferring of the Freedom on MacDiarmid would be unpopular in the burgh and was unlikely for that reason.

MacDiarmid wrote to the town clerk: 'Please inform your council that, if at any time they should offer me the Freedom, I will refuse it, and will also refuse any other public recognition offered me by Langholm.'

The *enfant terrible* died on 9 September 1978, aged eighty-six. He was buried in Langholm kirkyard (his widow, Valda Grieve, assured me 'out of spite' – she died 23 May 1989), and his mourners consisted of hundreds of people from around the world. It must have been too dreich a day for the Muckle Toon dignitaries, for they were conspicuous by their absence.

The Scotsman's obituary writer wrote that MacDiarmid's hot and angry integrity had radiated through Scotland for half a century. 'It burned holes in the blankets of national complacency, and it warmed those who often felt that their own country was a tundra in which the creators must freeze to death.'

Dumfries journalist Douglas Rome put it nicely when he described the great man as 'a Marxist of the Groucho fashion' who was the very emblem of Socrates's statement that life proceeded by paradox. Wrote Rome: 'His art was a knife that cut through Scotland's anglicised mask and the shrouds of dead centuries to free a fierce beauty.'

MacDiarmid had asked for his epitaph to be 'A disgrace to the community'. Instead, his gravestone reiterates the immortal quatrain from his masterpiece, *A Drunk Man Looks at the Thistle:*

> I'll ha'e nae hauf-way hoose, but aye be whaur
> Extremes meet – it's the only way I ken
> To dodge the curst conceit o' bein' richt
> That damns the vast majority o' men.

Ten years and a day after his death, the Annan branch of the Scottish National Party organised a wreath-laying ceremony (MacDiarmid was a co-founder of the party). A wreath in the shape of a Saltire cross studded with four little white roses was laid at the foot of his memorial in recognition of his famous lines:

> The rose of all the world is not for me.
> I want for my part
> Only the little white rose of Scotland,
> That smells sharp and sweet –
> And breaks the heart.

Ironically, I could hardly find the MacDiarmid Memorial on the day of the ceremony, and had to be pointed to 'yon metal thing' by a man in a fraying ex-Army sweater who had never heard of 'whitsisname, Dermott?' Irony number two: I had no bother locating another memorial – that of Sir John Malcolm, a former governor of Bombay and ambassador to Persia. MacDiarmid had penned the following lines about the slim obelisk on Whita Hill:

> Few ken to whom this muckle monument stands,
> Some general or admiral, I've nae doot
> On the hill-top whaur weather lang syne
> Has blotted its inscribed palaver oot.

Irony number three had been the opposition of the Common Riding committee to the siting of the MacDiarmid Memorial where it would interfere with 'the glorious view from the site enjoyed by natives and visitors alike during the hound trail'. MacDiarmid had been one of the Common Riding's staunchest supporters.

Eventually the Earl of Dalkeith provided an alternative site, and irony number four. MacDiarmid, you see, had always expressed his loathing for the gentry.

Fifth irony: at an auction to raise money for the memorial, MacDiarmid's pipe was sold to an aficionado of Sir Harry Lauder (the pipe had also been owned by Lauder). Need it be said how odd it is that Lauder, a man who preached the cult of tartanry, should help contribute to the memory of a man who despised it?

It turned out that Neil Armstrong, the first man on the moon and one with Borders blood in his veins, became the first Freeman of Langholm. He was feted by the inhabitants of Langholm's corridors of power at the Freedom ceremony in March 1972. Thousands lined the streets to hear him say that he would always treat Langholm as his home. He was later whisked off to spend the night with the Duke of Buccleuch at Drumlanrig Castle, near Thornhill.

Thomas Telford, whom the poet Robert Southey called the Colossus of Roads, has more kudos in Eskdale than MacDiarmid. The world's most famous bridge-builder was born in Westerkirk in 1757, the son of a poor shepherd. Laughing Tam who became known as *Pontifex Maximus* was apprenticed to a mason in Lochmaben and built the houses in New Langholm. He also built Langholm Bridge, where his mason's mark can still be seen on the stones. Telford's *piece de*

Neil Armstrong, the first man to step on the moon, the day he became the first Freeman of Langholm *(Courtesy: Robin Bryden)*

resistance was the Caledonian Canal, and he constructed many toll bars throughout Britain. He chose to be buried in Westminster Abbey among the élite.

Telford left a legacy of £1000 for the Langholm library, which still stands on the High Street as a monument to him. Coincidentally, the young Christopher Murray Grieve was brought up in a room below the library and used to brag of having read 12 000 of its books by the time he was fourteen. He brought them to his study by the washing-basketful.

Telford also endowed the Jamestown library, which was built to educate the minds of the miners of Britain's first antimony mine. On a map of the Scottish Borders Jamestown looks little bigger than a freckle on the eastern fringe of Dumfriesshire. The only house left standing now is the holiday home of a Warwickshire family, although Jamestown was once home to forty workers and their families. A couple of slag heaps and a waterlogged mineshaft are the only remaining clues to Jamestown's historic past.

The village was built by the Westerhall Mining Company, which proved enlightened for its time. Long before Karl Marx was lamenting the lot of the working classes, Jamestown miners earned ten shillings a week for their backache, and the company built a school for the children. The miners were allowed to graze their cows on the estate for a pound a year; and another ten bob was charged per acre of land for growing cabbages and potatoes. The laird, Sir James Johnstone, who was an MP, also built a winter store for grain, buying it in cheaply during the summer in order to dole it out at cost price to the workers in times of famine.

There was also a welfare fund catering for old age and ill health, and following the example set by Leadhills, the company built a library, giving the miners an initial £15 to buy books.

Jamestown was booming at the beginning of the ninteenth century, but transport problems shut the mines. There were to be two attempts to resurrect the industry, but the cost of moving the ore proved prohibitive, despite the later advantage of the Waverley rail line from Carlisle to Edinburgh, which closed amid howls of protest in 1968.

Jamestown library had a luckier fate than the miners who nurtured it – thanks to the Telford bequest. It was said last century to be the largest and best subscription library in the British Isles. It was later moved to the village of Bentpath.

One of the most unusual aspects of Jamestown library was its opening hours: it was open only once a month during the full moon. As recently as 1974, the librarian turned up on the appointed moonlit night between seven and nine o'clock to issue books to the twelve remaining active members.

Westerkirk has more fascinating lore. Legend has it that a Pictish king called Schaw is buried a stone's throw from Jamestown. It is supposed he drowned at the junction of the Black and White Esks (at the spot thenceforth known as King's Pool). The ancient custom of handfasting was enacted here, and at the annual fair, unmarried folk could choose their partners and try them out for a year. If they were pleased with

A rural scene near Jamestown

each other, they continued living in harmony. If not they parted and the fruit of their trial marriage went to the disaffected person. After their year was up, a peripatetic priest confirmed their marriage at the next handfasting fair. They called the man of God 'Book i' Bosom' because of the Bible he carried at all times under his cassock.

Just outisde Langholm on the B709 road overlooking a splendid tract of land called 'the Gates of Eden' you will come across a mansion with a unique collection of oddities ranging from Benin rattle-staffs to Sri Lankan carvings and prehistoric Red Indian pipes. The Craigcleuch Explorers' Museum houses a bewildering array of tribal treasures, and it is steadily attracting its fair share of tourists conducting their own exploraton of the beautiful Borders country. When I visited Craigcleuch, the former family home of Dumfries Tory MP Sir Hector Monro, an American traveller caused a stir when she said that a huge whale's ear-bone looked like the face of Richard Nixon, the former US president. It has to be admitted there is a distinct resemblance.

CHAPTER 5

The Road to Little Tibet

Castle O'er near Eskdalemuir is now besieged by conifer squadrons, although in ancient times it was a Roman fort which was the key to all the defences in the valleys. Some say it belonged to a Celtic warrior called *Lywarch Hen;* others believe it is Saxon in origin. What is known is that last century – before the advent of trees from Alaska – Castle O'er was the home of one Richard Bell, the first ostrich farmer in Britain.

Bell also bred rheas, cassowaries, snakes and monkeys. His exotic menagerie did produce some comic moments, as when his prize emu, Tommy, escaped one day and led a bevy of farmhands on a twenty-mile chase which was to be described locally as 'certainly equal to any foxhunt on record up to that day'. A rhea followed suit a few days later, which made Tommy's truancy pale into insignificance. She scampered and was at large for a fortnight after fighting off all the collie dogs from within a ten-mile radius of Langholm. Bell eventually enticed the escapee into a sack by means of a scone, but she ate her way out of confinement; and – as if in some slapstick movie – made off like a racehorse 'legs and airms a' wallopin' '. Had the ostrich craze survived into the twentieth century, ostrich steeplechases might have gone down well as an added attraction at the Langholm Common Riding. 'Come, see the world's largest birds, ridden by local jockeys', the papers might have declared.

Ronnie Rose has no ostriches, but he has plenty of other wildlife, and as wildlife manager for the Economic Forestry Group (EFG) in the largest area of private plantations in Britain, he has proved that evergreen need not mean ever-boring. Ronnie, a pugnacious Highlander whose father and grandfather were stalkers to the Royal family at Balmoral, has turned normally sombre swathes of exotic softwoods into havens for flora and fauna – and earned himself a Churchill Fellowship and a world-wide reputation as an environmentalist into the bargain. From the top of his deerstalker hat to the feet at the bottom of his plus-fours, he is every millimetre a

Ronnie Rose, wildlife manager for the Economic Forestry Group *(Courtesy: The Scotsman Publications Ltd)*

dedicated researcher, and his laboratory stretches over several thousand acres of Borders scenery. His experiment has lasted since 1970. By 1988 he and his wildlife management team had increased the number of species of birds in the EFG's forest at Eskdalemuir from thirty-three to 107. The deer population had started off a sickly six, and expanded to 3000 'stoatirs'.

The Rose experiment led to the reopening of a hotel and a general revitalisation of the rural economy of this former hill sheep farming valley. Surviving sheep farmers agree not to shoot Ronnie's deer, and in turn he controls predators. It is also a stipulation that visitors who come to Eskdalemuir to shoot (there's a three-year waiting list) seek lodgings with local farmers.

Ronnie also runs an interpretation centre which is visited by 2000 Borders school children per year. There he tells them about his method of allowing Nature to be self-regulating and about his design of forests which allows wildlife to thrive.

Never a man to mince his words, he tells them that he has challenged herbicide representatives to drink their wares in front of him or else go thither – and only one eager salesman has taken up the challenge. They tell me he is still alive, and going up in the sales world.

Three out of four kestrels and tawny owls at Eskdalemuir nest in home-made boxes. And merlins and peregrine falcons are now well-established owing to the number of small birds and the food chain provided by the forest design. When I went for a walk with Ronnie up the woods, he pointed up to a can jammed into a tree: 'That's the only good use for a bloody chemical can – for nesting.'

Ronnie created a series of natural pools at Eskdalemuir, but the burrowing of water voles threatened the stability of the dam. Pellet analysis showed that the resident short-eared owls preferred short-tailed voles as a delicacy. 'They not only loved voles, they bloody well loved sitting on poles', declared the kenspeckle figure. 'So we attracted them all the way to the pond by putting up three posts and moving them weekly nearer and nearer the pond.'

It worked: the owls took to water voles as readily as they had consumed their cousins, and now there are thirty pairs of short-eared owls at Eskdalemuir, which thrive on a varied regimen.

Whether you are sitting nursing a piping mug of coffee in Ronnie's house at Burncleuch or trying to take shorthand notes as he aims his four-wheel drive Japanese motor at seemingly unnegotiable gradients in the wilds, Ronnie Rose comes across as a fascinating character. The last I heard of him he had successfully persuaded a Yugoslavian professor to preach the Rose philosophy in his country.

Ronnie chuckled over the telephone: 'He tells me he will be persuading his superiors to build wee bloody Eskdalemuirs up and down Slovenia. It's heartwarming and makes the job worthwhile, but in many areas of Britain, foresters are prepared to make do with part-time pest controllers. We must educate the public about this, and root out the irresponsible in our profession. These so-called experts are no more than usherettes at a film called Disaster.'

Dumfries and Galloway region is already the most heavily

afforested in Britain. And Ronnie Rose's methods are rare. Afforestation in Galloway has ruined the area for hillwalkers, and the same is happening in the Moffat hills and Ettrick Valley. Prince Charles, the President of the Royal Forestry Society, said in 1983 that the dense areas of Sitka Spruce in Dumfries and Galloway left much to be desired as wildlife habitats.

The situation will probably get worse, since Dumfries and Galloway Regional Council is on record as favouring afforestation. In fact the Scottish Woodland Owners' Association told the council in 1985 that they recommended planting a further 40 000 hectares – which would bring the total area of the region under the bottle-green softwoods to twenty-seven per cent. The council convener, John Jameson, expressed the council's support for increased afforestation, saying they had 'the ideal climate for silviculture'.

Meanwhile, Ordnance Survey maps of Dumfries and Galloway continue to become increasingly – and frustratingly – out of date.

If ostriches, handfasting and Alaskan fir-trees sound offbeat, then maroon-robed monks are not what you would expect to see in a southern Scottish rural community. But the tranquillity of Samye Ling Tibetan Centre has attracted many searchers of enlightenment since 1967, when two monks who had fled the Chinese invasion of their homeland, took over Johnstone House mansion at Eskdalemuir. It was the first Tibetan Buddhist monastery in the western world, and many famous and not so famous people have 'hitched' their way up to 'little Tibet' via the twisting road from Lockerbie and Boreland or over the other route from Langholm via Westerkirk.

The centre was the focus of world press coverage in 1984 when His Holiness the Dalai Lama, the exiled 'God-king of Tibet' visited it and boosted the campaign inviting the public to lay a brick of the new temple for a pound.

On 26 March 1989, forty people from all walks of life began four years' solitary confinement in a 'time capsule' at Samye Ling. The twenty men and twenty women have chosen to turn their backs on society and to devote their lives to prayer and meditation alone. They are to be allowed no newspapers, no

The Rt Hon David Steel MP at the opening of the Samye Ling Tibetan temple, Eskdalemuir on 8 August 1988 *(Photograph: Steve Matthew, Annan)*

television, no radio, no telephones and no visitors. They are to get up at 4.00 am after only five hours' sleep. The group, which includes a high order Tibetan lama, will only emerge before the four years are up to pray for mankind in the event of a major disaster.

Life is ordinarily no dawdle for the Buddhists of Samye Ling: work and prayers start with a rising bell at 5.45 am, and the strenuous day does not end until 10.00 pm.

From one Ayrshire cow called Daisy, the Buddhist colony has expanded its herd to fifteen: marshland has been drained for grazing, and a byre, a dairy complex, hay barn and midden were completed in the mid 1980s. The monks make cheese, yoghurt and butter. Vegetarian food is grown on an acre and a half of ground. The produce is praised annually by kirk elders, farmers and other local people at the open day.

There's a thriving printing centre which turns out beautifully illustrated cards, Tibetan prayers, posters, stationery and books. The resident artist, Sherapalden Beru, born in 1910, is the leading master in the Karma Gadri tradition, and his Thangka paintings hang in the new temple which was his brainchild and which opened in August 1988.

The centre offers two-day sessions including meditation, art therapy, retreat and study for Buddhists and non-Buddhists. It is a registered charity, totally dependent on fees from guests, who come to seek a retreat from the rat race.

The aforesaid temple, Europe's largest, was opened by David Steel, the former Liberal leader, on the eighth day of the eighth month in 1988, the luckiest day of the decade. His constituency begins over the county boundary. He was dressed for the occasion in the raiment of a Privy councillor originally worn by a member of the Lloyd George cabinet. Religious and cultural differences would have been forgotten but for a Jedburgh fundamentalist who rode in on a motorbike and confronted rabbis, monks, Kirk ministers and Hindu adepts. He waved a placard proclaiming that it was Covenanting country and denounced Buddhism in the Borders. He was stopped from demonstrating further by the police.

David Steel told onlookers that Buddhism was the epitome of tolerance and compassion, two qualities which were sadly lacking in present-day society.

All has not been rosy, though, between the native Lowlanders and the incoming Buddhists. Some of the indigenous rustics believe that the Tibetans and 'hingers-on' have taken over the valley by stealth, imposed an alien culture, and bought up every possible square inch of land in the area. The 'us and them' situation came to a dramatic head in 1988 when administrators at the centre announced plans for a crematorium there. At a public meeting in the village hall, one objector said that the insidious spread of the Centre's influence far and wide had been watched with growing concern. 'One hopes that nightmarish visions of the White Esk becoming a smaller version of the River Ganges can be dismissed,' he said, before declaring that the narrow road to the monastery would become jammed with 'rows of funeral corteges queuing up for their twenty minutes' worth.'

Eskdalemuir Observatory, which was opened in 1908 because London trams had been interfering with the magnetic recording equipment at Kew, is within a mile of Samye Ling.

And its superintendent, David Moore, indicated his concern at the implications of a crematorium. The observatory is one of ten pollution monitoring stations in Scotland, and the burning of bodies down the road would have interfered with pollution statistics. The station is the only one in Britain which measures 'turbidity' for the World Meteorological Office, and fumes would have hovered between measuring equipment and the sun.

In the end, Samye Ling withdrew their planning application, so there are no longer prospects of a crematorium in the Border hills. However, in 1989, Samye Ling were having informal talks with the Scottish Tourist Board with a view to opening a visitor centre to tell the story of Tibet's religious, artistic and cultural heritage. A spokesman for the Dumfries and Galloway Tourist Board said that the Centre was now more disposed to tourism development because of the amount of interest it had generated in the year of the opening of the temple.

She added: 'It is worth pointing out, however, that the impression received from comments from some of the local residents, is one of concern regarding the scale of development of such a centre, and whether it would take over the valley.'

SECTION 2: *THE SOLWAY COAST*

CHAPTER 6

Bridge Over Troubled Water

When it opened in 1869 it was the longest bridge in Europe; it was a mile and 200 yards long; it united the countries of Scotland and England. The Solway Viaduct ran from Annan on the Scottish side to Bowness on the English side – or rather in the reverse direction, since it was built to convey iron ore from West Cumberland to the smelters of Lanarkshire and avoid the snarl-up at Carlisle.

The viaduct, all 5000 tons of it, was part of the Solway Junction railway which ran from Brayton on the outskirts of Kirkbride in Cumberland over the treacherous firth to Annan and then to the main line at Kirtlebridge in Annandale. Shawhill station in Annan – now a scrapyard – was built to serve the line. Chapelcross discharge pipeline runs through.

The bridge spanned the Solway by means of 197 piers, and the foundations were sunk forty feet into the sea-bed. Oddly, there was a legal wrangle with and between the owners of the foreshores, the Earl of Lonsdale in England and the Crown Commissioners in southern Scotland (Who owned the sea-bed?). Nine years after the line opened, its owners, the Solway Junction Railway Company – who were heavily backed by Caledonian – paid £105 to the Commissioners.

The construction, hailed as 'a gallant monument to an age of reckless enterprise' after its demolition in 1935, was designed by James Brunlees (who was later knighted). He also drew up the plans for Southend pier and was a consultant on the abortive Channel Tunnel plan of the 1880s.

The Solway Viaduct's fame has been eclipsed by its brothers, the Tay and Forth Bridges, but it had a chequered history of its own. It first opened for freight in September 1869, and to passengers in July 1870; there were four passenger trains each way every day. But, despite the inherent charm of journeying by train over the sea from England to Scotland, the line lost

Solway Viaduct before it was destroyed

money. Among the reasons were the increasing importations of foreign ore and the improvements made in local smelting in Cumberland.

Disaster struck in January 1881 – not a disaster on the scale of the Tay Bridge in 1879 – but a disaster for the line itself. Forty-five of its piers were wrecked by gigantic ice floes, one of which is said to have measured twenty-seven yards by two.

The line soldiered on, though. But it eventually shut down on 1 September 1921, although the company, based on the Isle of Wight, still existed. London Midland and Scottish (LMS) took it on in 1923, and barriers went up to stop folk walking across it. Bowness was just over a mile over the water for thirsty Scotsmen who defied death on the occasional Sunday to take advantage of the more liberal licensing regulations in England.

Drunkards were not the only chancers. In an article for Dumfriesshire Newspapers a few years ago, Thomas Jackson of Moffat wrote: 'A chum of my sister attending Annan Academy from Bowness, and who previously travelled by train, now walked across each school-day until accommodated elsewhere.

Solway Viaduct after the disaster

'Furthermore, many a Scottish Border Romeo slipped secretly across the Solway Viaduct to keep rendezvous with his fair English Juliet.'

Incidentally, Jackson's father bought one of the old Solway Junction signal-boxes. It stood in a modified form in their garden at Gretna Green – acting as a greenhouse.

Jackson senior had been involved in the dismantling of the viaduct from 1934 to 1935. Even that was fraught with problems. Salmon stake-net fishermen were aghast when LMS tried to blow up the boulders which protected the foundations from one of the fastest tides in Europe. And in the end railway surfacemen shifted them with great difficulty at low tide.

In the 1960s the line of the old viaduct was the cornerstone of an ambitious plan for an atomic megalopolis which would have straddled the Solway Firth and dramatically changed the face of Dumfriesshire. According to Robert Drew, a nuclear physicist at Chapelcross Nuclear Power Station near Annan, the area between Dumfries and Carlisle was 'the crossroads of the nation'. And in 1964 he saw the Solway as 'a nuclear powerhouse and international demonstration area for ideas and patterns that together constitute a viable and civilised twentieth-century ecology for mankind, that is an environment for living fully balanced between human needs and natural resources'.

Annan might now have had a space-age university, a shopping precinct resembling that of Sauchiehall Street, Glasgow, and four nuclear power stations cooled by millions of gallons of water from the Solway Firth. Surplus energy from the firth was to have heated many acres of market gardens along the Lochar Moss 'to a Mediterranean soil climate'. Hovercraft would have tripped to Cumberland and back, as ferries had done the previous century. *The Times Review of Industry and Technology* wrote that Drew's plan was so big it would go from pigeon-hole to in-tray for the rest of his life. Yet a Government White Paper on the Scottish Economy (1966) stated that the area between Dumfries and Carlisle (and Annan is bang in the middle) might well take a large development of city size in the closing decade of the century. Drew also saw scope for a major international airport at Solway City. He wrote: 'Looking at the strategic placement of the Solway at the hub and centre of a wheel which has as its rim Glasgow, Edinburgh, Newcastle, Teesside and Lancaster, is it entirely fanciful to suggest that no better location could be found for another international airport, which is almost certain to be needed within twenty years?'

Drew's plan had the technocrats dancing. Many scientists were impressed. The firm Alcan even sponsored a similar scheme for a circuit-linear city for 50 000 people from Annan to Gretna and over the Solway to Bowness (along the line of the old viaduct) and back to Annan. The Drew blueprint was supported by every university within a 150-mile radius of Annan, and it was backed by Sir Edwin, now Lord, McAlpine, and Viscount Stormont, now Lord Mansfield. Comlongon Castle was to have been a 'Regional Resource Development Institute'.

But Drew's project was shelved when the Labour Government came to power and Harold Wilson was reluctant to spend money on research. A watered-down version was wheeled out of the archives after the Chernobyl explosion in 1986, at the suggestion of Labour MP Dale Campbell-Savours. He called for a barrage to be built across the Solway to reduce the country's reliance on nuclear power. Conservationists leapt to the offensive, and the Solway was listed by the Royal Society for the Protection of Birds as an estuary in peril.

There was to be no Solway City. Stansted in the Home Counties got the airport, Sizewell got the atom plants, and the Channel was the location for a tunnel which Drew had envisaged for the Irish Sea. According to Drew it would have cost an initial £20 million for a project aimed at communication, energy conservation, water supply and land reclamation; and he later criticised the Government for spending £120 million on the Kielder Dam in the North of England – a single-purpose project.

Nowadays the Solway Firth is a comparatively quiet place – rather than the polluted outlet of a metropolis, if you forget the emissions from Sellafield which make it the dustbin of Europe. Where Sir Walter Scott pitched the smuggling scenes of *Redgauntlet* and horsemen used to stage salmon-spearing competitions with leisters, oil magnates were in the 1980s drilling for oil below the sea-bed. Disappointing survey findings led London-based Enterprise Oil to relinquish their exploratory licence covering the inner estuary. There was nothing to suggest viable reserves of oil and gas, according to a company spokesman. The company had also taken the area's scenic beauty and environmental sensitivity into consideration, he said.

A dwindling band of netsmen ekes out a living in the Solway. Stake-netters are not only the victims of a declining number of salmon but also they are cited in official reports as the people most at risk from radioactivity.

Haaf-net fishing, River Nith, Solway Estuary, Dumfriesshire
(Photograph: Werner Kissling, 1957 © School of Scottish Studies)

Haaf-netting, a form peculiar to the Solway, is under threat from a different element: the authorities. Annan's forty-six licensed fishermen unanimously signed a petition in December 1988 calling upon English bailliffs to keep to their own side of the border – amid a public debate about the legality of haaf-netting. They contended that the cross-border incursions were part of a politically motivated move to secure test-cases against haaf-netters in Scottish courts – an attempt by rich landowners to stop working-class people fishing in local waters.

Haaf-netting had been carried on in the firth since the days of the Vikings (Glencaple, once a flourishing shipbuilding centre, and Annan were the strongholds). In Annan, King James VI's charter of 1612 permits the locals to net in a designated area.

Policemen, local government officers and councillors are among those who still carry out the haaf-netting – although those who wrote up the Salmon Act 1986, failed to list it as a legitimate form of fishing. The act vests power in the Secretary of State for Scotland 'after consulting such persons as he considers appropriate to make regulations with respect to obstructions in rivers or estuaries to the passage of salmon'.

According to Samuel Adamson, of the Annan Fishermen's Association: 'Such people as the Government considers appropriate might mean riparian landowners, who dominate Annan Fishery Board.'

Anglers claim netters wipe estuaries clean of fish, but netters deny this, pointing to the enjoyment factor as the motivating force, rather than the quantity of fish.

Haaf-netters stand up to their breasts in the channel of the estuary forming a human chain. They stand against the current holding their strange-looking net and frame. If a salmon is caught in the right 'poke', the netter flings it with his right hand over into the double yarn. He then turns with his back to the tide and knocks the fish out with his mallet.

Haaf-netting is known to require considerable strength and courage. A man may stand just too long to escape the pressing flood and be washed away before he can get to the brow of the channel. It is said that few haaf-netters are able to swim.

Threats to fishermen are nothing new. Centuries ago, Sir James Graham of Netherby built a cauld across the River Esk – which stopped salmon entering the Scottish side of the estuary. According to Brian Blake in his book *The Solway Firth*: 'In this dilemma, the Scots people assembled in numbers by signal of rocket-lights, and widely armed with fowling-pieces, fish spears, and such rustic weapons, marched to the banks of the river for the purpose of pulling down the dam-dyke objected to.'

Sir James saw sense, though – and made a hole in the dyke which eventually the river swept away.

CHAPTER 7

Atomic Annan

Annan is an enigma happed up in a riddle. A frontier town with an absorbingly interesting past, it used to be called the 'Queen of the Border'. But the town has lost much of its regality over the years and has an air about it which is not easily explained by the fact that its ancient subjects had to be doughty fighters, owing to their unenviable position in the front-line against the English. Enigmatic? What other town in the south of Scotland has such history but has failed so abysmally to capitalise on its assets?

The celebrated African explorer, Hugh Clapperton, was born in Butts Street; Thomas Carlyle was educated at the old Academy in the High Street, and the famous evangelist, Edward Irving, was born and bred in the town. Bonnie Prince Charlie marched through in 1745, and King Robert the Bruce's ancestors had their stronghold adjacent to where the town hall now stands.

Shipwrights from the Welldale in Annan turned out some of the world's most famous clippers, and local masons hewed the sandstone which was shipped to New York for the base of the Statue of Liberty.

Sir Walter Scott's *Redgauntlet* and *Guy Mannering* feature Annan, and the poet Robert Burns worked the Solway as an exciseman. Yet this once prosperous seaport is not even on the official Solway Coast Heritage Trail. Till now the authorities have been content to rely on the shaky prosperity derived from Scotland's oldest nuclear power station whose four cooling-towers dominate the landscape for miles around.

Late twentieth century man's proneness to stress, if not tourism, has benefited the community. For the drug conglomerate, Glaxochem, moved into neighbouring Newbie in 1979. NEI Cochran, also of Newbie, were going through a rough patch at the time of writing, although they had built the world's first submarine and some of the units for Mulberry Harbour, which was used in the D-Day landings. A Cochran boiler had once been a household name, but the bubble had burst.

Annandale and Eskdale District Council finally opened a new toilet block in Annan in 1989, and not before time: a year and a bit beforehand, the town's toilets had been voted, by desperate travellers in a Radio Scotland phone-in, Scotland's worst.

In winter, Annan is a dour place: most Scottish towns, I suppose, are. But the sandstone buildings give off a pleasing, rosy hue in the late summer sunlight. On the negative side, summer's the time when there's more through-traffic to add to the lorries and juggernauts which trundle over the bridge on their way to the Irish ferry at Stranraer. The town, none the less, is to be by-passed by the autumn of 1989. And here's where the trouble will begin: unless the authorities see it as a challenge or incentive, the town will become another of those familiar ghost-towns we all read about in obscure magazines.

Tourism? In the same year the by-pass is due for completion, British Nuclear Fuels (BNFL) announce that they are starting a feasibility study into the future of the thirty-year-old Magnox nuclear plant – and one of the options is a replacement station up to three times the size of the existing one.

Chapelcross was opened on a disused aerodrome at Creca in 1959 to produce weapons-grade plutonium, electricity being a sideline. A tritium plant came on line in 1980, despite fierce opposition (predictably from outsiders).

BNFL continued to buy every piece of land in the area they could, and Neville Chamberlain, their chairman, declared in 1989 that the Chapelcross site had space and resources and was near to a major point in the national grid. He added: 'We believe that it makes sense to examine the possibility of developing Chapelcross thoroughly and professionally before making any decision.'

For the record, I believe, in the words of the late Scottish Nationalist lawyer, Willie Macrae: 'Ye dinnae keep pigs till ye ken where ye're gaun to pit their shite.'

BNFL had tried to win a contract for an interim dry buffer store at Chapelcross, but they lost it to Heysham in Lancashire. Annandale and Eskdale District Council – one of only three local authorities in Scotland controlled by the Social and Liberal Democrats – were disappointed, having backed the

Old Annan

prospect of what many people saw as a nuclear 'coup' which would have put paid to any chances of attracting tourists to Annan.

Officially, Chapelcross has an excellent safety record, and has won a string of awards. Doubts, though, persist. In 1984, a Yorkshire TV documentary revealed that young children took regular summer showers below the outlet of the pipeline from Chapelcross into the Solway Firth; and a geiger counter showed unacceptably high readings. Official figures for 1987 show a higher than average rate of childhood leukaemia within a 12.5 kilometre radius of the site. And a survey of the incidence of the disease in Dumfries and Galloway was launched in 1988 by Dr Francis Toolis of Dumfries, following concern expressed about clusters around nuclear sites.

The cynic could say that Annan still suffers from a curse laid on it by an Irish saint 800 years ago. St Malachy, who became Archbishop of Armagh, cursed the Bruces and their town after they failed to spare the life of a condemned thief at Malachy's bidding.

Subsequently, the course of the River Annan – on which the town stands – was altered by an unknown disaster, with devastating results. Part of the castle motte was washed away, and the Bruces and all their satellites flitted to Lochmaben.

Last remnant of Annan Castle: The Brus Stane with the inscription 'Robert de Brus, Counte d Carrick et seityur du val de Anann, An° 1300' *(Courtesy: Annan Riding of the Marches Publications)*

Around the same time, a plague-spreading vampire is said to have run amok in Annan. Reportedly, he came from Bruce's lands in Yorkshire and was buried in the local kirkyard, but refused to bide there. Apparently, he was at last released from the living dead by two Annanites who dug his body up, hacked his heart out with a wooden shovel and threw it on to a bonfire.

The vampire legend is unsubstantiated, but that of Malachy is supported by the *Lanercost Chronicle,* which states: 'Robert the Bruce rests with his ancestors in Guisborough in England, but it was in Annan that he yielded up his spirit – the chief town which lost its dignity as a burgh through the curse of a just man.'

On his return from crusading in the Holy Land in 1273, Robert Bruce (the Competitor) stopped off at St Malachy's tomb at Clairvaux in France and made peace with the saint by setting up three silver lamps which were to burn for ever at his grave. The curse appeared to lift: the fortunes of the Bruces took an upward swing. The Competitor's grandson was crowned King of Scotland after stabbing the Red Comyn in Dumfries.

Edward Balliol was installed as puppet-king when Bruce died, but he came a cropper at the hands of a gang of Annan patriots who attacked his camp on the burgh moor. It is recorded that the 'miserable mimic of a king' galloped half-naked on an unsaddled cart-horse, which did not stop until it was on English soil.

Malachy's body rested in peace for some 600 years, illuminated by the lamps of the Lords of Annandale. Then came the French Revolution, in the turmoil of which his tomb was desecrated.

Opinions about Annan have been many and varied. The town reminded Dorothy Wordsworth of France and Germany ('many of the houses large and gloomy, the size of them outrunning their comforts'). A different view was expressed by the travel writer Richard Ayton ten years later. (He incidentally gauged the number of whisky drinkers in town by the inordinately large number of red noses.) Ayton noticed huts on the High Street and recorded: 'One is not surprised at seeing such kind of habitation among the wilds of the mountains, where every man builds his own house in a Robinson Crusoe-like manner, with any makeshift materials and tools that he can find, but I should really scarcely have expected to find them in a land of bricks and mortar.'

The philanthropist Andrew Carnegie lunched in the town in 1882 during his tour of Britain, and he studied the bridge built by Thomas Carlyle's father, calling it 'an honest brig designed to stand and never shame the builder'.

Carlyle himself did not warm to Annan. He described his early days as a schoolboy there as a 'doleful and hateful life'. From the 'red sunny Whitsuntide morning' in 1806 when his father walked him to school from their home in Ecclefechan until the day he walked to Edinburgh University three years later, he was bullied by his colleagues and thumped by Adam Hope, his teacher.

The embryonic 'Sage of Chelsea' taught in Annan. In 1988, the regional council was poised to convert his old school, the Hinterschlag Gymnasium of *Sartor Resartus,* into sheltered housing. The late David Patterson, who had owned it and whom I had known quite well, would have turned in his grave. It would have been the perfect place for a museum of local history.

Carlyle's friend, Edward Irving, would have figured in that

museum. For he was, as de Quincey put it, 'the greatest orator of his time'. Irving was born in 1792 in a house near the Fish Cross, and his statue, which was originally erected outside the town hall, can now be seen in the precincts of Annan Old Kirk. Ironically, Irving was, after a trial in the church, excommunicated from Annan Presbytery in 1833 for heresy.

According to Tennyson, Irving was:

> No sabbath drawler of old saws,
> Distilled from some worm-cankered homily,
> But spurred at heart with fiercest energy
> To embattail and to wail about his cause
> With iron-worded proof.

Hugh Clapperton was another noted Annanite who would have been mentioned in the museum. In his *Sketches from Nature,* John McDiarmid wrote that, had Clapperton stuck to the coasting trade in America, instead of becoming an explorer, he would have finally retired to Annan with a fortune and 'vegetated tranquilly for ten or twenty years, reading newspapers or playing billiards in the forenoon, and smoking cigars and drinking whisky-punch in the evenings'.

As it was, Clapperton died of jungle fever at the age of thirty-nine in a mud hut in Sokoto so near and yet so far from determining the course of the River Niger. His body was carted by camel five miles outside Sokoto and buried there. According to his servant, Richard Lander: 'Not a single soul listened to this peculiarly distressing ceremony, for the slaves were quarrelling with each other the whole time it lasted.' A plaque in Annan town hall next to the famous Brus Stane lists the explorer's accomplishments. He also has a street in town named after him.

Annan was Robert Burns's 'Blinkin' Bess o' Annandale that dwelt by Solwayside', and he stayed there to keep an eye out for smugglers in a town which was fair hotchin' with them. Burns lodged with a future Provost called Thomas Williamson, whose house occupied the site where the Café Royal now stands. One night there was a big gathering at the house, and the poet excused himself saying he was going for a dander. On his return from the Annan Bridge, Burns penned the words of 'The De'il's awa wi' the Exciseman', and earned himself loud

Hugh Clapperton *(Source: Annandale & Eskdale District Council, Photograph: Alister Lynn, Annan)*

cheers when he recited the poem. A stone plaque on the side of the chip shop records the historic event.

But for the Annan-born minister Thomas Blacklock, Burns would have emigrated to Jamaica, and Scotland would have lost its number one bard. Blacklock, who had been struck blind by smallpox as an infant, had been ordained to the Church of Scotland, but his parishioners in Kirkcudbright complained about his handicap, whereupon he resigned and moved to Edinburgh. He later wrote a lampoon about the Galloway town called *Pistapolis,* which appeared in the *Scottish Historical Review.* He was also a noted poet and wrote a definition of the word 'blind' for the *Encyclopaedia Britannica.* According to Burns, he had 'a clear head and an excellent heart'.

Annan's William Nicol was another of Burns's cronies. A drinking buddie whom he referred to as 'kind, honest-hearted Willie', he was the man who brewed the famous 'peck o' maut'. Nicol, born in 1774 on Dumbretton farm (near where Chapelcross stands today), became classics master at Edinburgh's Royal High School. The letter which Burns wrote to him from Carlisle during his Border Tour is the only extant prose epistle in the Scots dialect.

From bards to barques: maritime affairs is another subject which would fill a local museum. Shipbuilding was the life-blood of Annan in the middle of last century when Nicholsons of Port Street turned out tea-clippers which were to sail the seven seas from Chile to China. One naval expert claimed the town's shipwrights were second to none in Scotland.

Shipbuilding was so important to the town that schoolchildren were given a holiday to see a clipper being launched, and the Dumfriesshire gentry would rattle down to the harbour in their carriages to see history in the making. People came from all over Scotland for the launch of a vessel, and the crowds were huge. Four thousand, for instance, gathered to see *The Annandale* take to the tide. The *Dumfries Standard* recorded the event as follows: 'High tide was about half past one o' clock, but long before that time, the immediate vicinity of the shipyard and the adjoining quay were crowded; the opposite bank too was lined with a living fringe, and about a hundred yards down the river, we could see a steamer from Maryport and the Annan steam-tug, each with a freight of spectators and each occasionally puffing and snorting – we are sure not contemptuously – as they waited for the advent of their young and gigantic sister.'

The Annandale was then the longest ship in the world, and her builder Ben Nicholson was a lad of only twenty-one. Ben, whose descendants still live along the Solway coast, had served his time in Liverpool which then had a close association with Annan, being 'jeest doon the watter'. His ship, however, a drawing of whose midship is lodged in the National Maritime Museum, was not to be a lucky one. Despite her glorious launch, severe weather made her maiden voyage from Liverpool to Bombay last nearly three years, and her next voyage was equally hapless. Ben Nicholson's brother's log reveals a tale of disaster and adversity featuring the death of the skipper, Captain Atchison and his burial at sea. *The Annandale* later ran aground in the United States and was condemned and sold.

The *Brooklyn Index* of New York called another Nicholson clipper, *Sarah Nicholson,* 'a marvel of neatness and a beautiful model'; and *The Queensberry,* another great clipper, took part in the tea races from Shanghai to London, sailing home 'in goodly company', though never quite winning. The captain's log of November 1858 maintained, however, that she had 'just surpassed the fastest ship afloat'.

The coming of the railways ended the golden days of Annan clippers (as it did Dumfries's and Glencaple's), and in 1868, the shipbuilding shed was sold to a firm in Carlisle. It was the last melancholy memento of the days when the sound of ship carpenters' mallets had rung across the harbour.

Annan's affair with the sea survives in her fishermen, themselves a dying breed, although a revival in the sprat industry was recorded in 1988. At one time a lighthouse-keeper cycled out from Annan to Barnkirk Point at dusk to light the lamps of the lighthouse, stayed overnight and pedalled back the following morning, but it was demolished in the 1950s in the interests of post-war economy. A remote-controlled lamp on a pole was put in its place.

Annan also once had thriving bacon-curing and cotton industries, and Provost Oats put the town on the map. The famous oats were made in the town's mills by Robert Robinson and Sons, one of whose partners, William Robinson, was a Provost of Annan (Robinson's house, aptly named Cereal House, is now inhabited by Frank Park, the Convener of Annandale and Eskdale District Council). The firm also manufactured tapioca and pulses – and a commodity called crisks, which were the result of an unsuccessful attempt to make breakfast cereal. They became a handy ingredient in sausages!

The town had three breweries and a distillery whose produce satisfied the thirsty farmhands who annually attended the hiring fairs on the High Street. Shows lined both sides of the street, but the fairs were stopped and moved to the Merse after a pedestrian was hit by a stray ball thrown at an Aunt Sally.

Extensive nurseries in Annan once provided employment for a hundred people (hence Nursery Place). Hundreds of thousands of saplings were shipped to America until high tariffs led to liquidation. Fieldside Nurseries, which produced 25 000 or more hybrid perpetual roses a year, occupied sixty acres.

Many Annandale families emigrated via Annan harbour to find work in the New World – at a time when two rival companies ran regular steamers to and from Liverpool, and ferries ran to and from Cumberland. The emigrants were bound for Canada, America, Australia, New Zealand or the Cape of Good Hope where huge fortunes could be amassed. A Lockerbie emigrant founded the town of Morrinsville, fifty miles from Auckland in New Zealand. And a man called George Johnston, whose early life in Annandale remains a mystery, was the first white Australian. Johnston, a twenty-six-year-old lieutenant in the Royal Marines, was first ashore when the First Fleet landed in Sydney Cove in 1788. He stepped ashore in a wig, red coat and white breeches on 26 January 1788, from the back of a barefooted convict who had carried him through the water. The Government granted him ninety acres of land which eventually became known as Annandale and is now a suburb of Sydney.

Some fortune-hungry people, however, never made it. Two Annan men went down with *The Thetis* off the coast of St Lawrence in Canada in 1870, and several Annan people were among the casualties in the Montreal steamship disaster in

Powfoot's redbrick houses *(Photograph: Alister Lynn, Annan)*

1857. Two years later, a Captain Andrew Johnstone of Ecclefechan and Andrew Aitchison of Annan were among the dead when the Royal Charter Australian Packet sank off Wales with £800 000 worth of gold on board.

And what of modern Annan? The by-pass will bring about a revolutionary change, and strenuous attempts will have to be made to attract tourism to the town. A step in that direction was the twinning of Annan with Watermael-Boitsfort, a suburb of Brussels, in 1988: the first international twinning involving a Dumfriesshire town. A historic charter-signing ceremony in the town hall was attended by twenty-one Belgian visitors. The connection between Annan and the Belgian capital was that the King's Own Scottish Borderers (KOSB) had helped liberate the city from Hitler. In April 1989, the KOSB received the Freedom of Annandale and Eskdale District to mark their 300th birthday.

There are also plans in the offing for a maritime museum in Port Street, and a multi-million pound harbour redevelopment

Ellerslie, Powfoot, backing on to the Pow Burn *(Photograph: Alister Lynn, Annan)*

project. 'Yuppies' seem to like converted docklands in which to live, and flats for this section of the populace appear a possibility.

Annan would not be worried now about tourism if plans hatched at the tail-end of last century for a 'Blackpool of the North' had been carried through. Powfoot, three miles west of Annan, was to be the new Blackpool. But it is now only a dormitory town, a second-class coastal resort with an ugly beach. Its houses, nevertheless, are quickly snapped up by the southern English when they come on the market, maybe because of the panoramic view of the Lakeland peaks across the water.

Powfoot's redbrick houses are unique in Scotland. They are of a Merseyside design: the work of two local lads o' pairts who served their time in Bootle and returned to transform Powfoot from a somnolent fishermen's village to a health resort. They acquired land from the Marquis of Queensberry and built a series of avenues.

Edward Brook, who took over Kinmount estate in 1896, was also a man with a vision and he had three miles of roads laid out to the Solway retreat. Plans were outlined for fifty acres of ornamental terraces and crescents, and he had the distinctive Queensberry Terrace at Cummertrees built in 1900. More houses were to stretch right up the foreshore, but they were never achieved.

Brook had already established a mile-long chain of artificial lakes, which became a fashionable tourist trap. They had islets, waterfalls and exotic shrubs, and they teemed with trout. One of the lakes was situated behind Cummertrees kirk and could be seen by travellers as they chugged into the railway station. Pleasure boats were to have been anchored at a Blackpool-style promenade, but the promenade did not materialise.

Notwithstanding the absence of a promenade, hundreds of bathers used to alight at the station and head either for the redbrick houses or to a series of huts called 'Chinatown', depending on their social status. 'Chinatown', along the shore towards Newbie, was pulled down when ICI built an explosives factory next to the shore. They were deemed a fire hazard.

Today most of the redbrick houses are listed buildings, and Queensberry Terrace is the last reminder that Powfoot could have been a bumper resort. Gone are the annual sand races held at Powfoot by the Cumberland Motor Cycle Club, when the tide was out. The lakes are an overgrown eyesore, although they have been earmarked as the site of a chalet complex. At an auction sale in 1986 the long-abandoned forecourt of Cummertrees station was eventually sold off.

CHAPTER 8

Ruthwell to Caerlaverock

Ruthwell's most humorous legend relates to a pig which gave some of the area's residents the 'holy willies'.

The tale of the 'grumphie' belonging to 'the Gudeman o' the Brow' sounds like a joke. But a self-respecting old London magazine documents it. The said 'gudeman' received the pig as a present from a foreign acquaintance. One day the animal, said to be the first of its kind in the south of Scotland, absconded across the River Lochar into the parish of Caerlaverock. A woman herding cattle ran for her life and fainted when she reached her home hamlet of Blackshaw. She told her family she had seen the devil coming out of the sea. It had come grunting and gaping up to her heels. The locals fled into byres, while a schoolmaster, deciding to act as exorcist, got out a Bible and a sword. But his hair stood on end when he saw the beast. Eventually, the village idiot informed everybody it was 'the Gudeman o' the Brow's grumphie', and fed it a meal of straw.

Suitably replenished, the swine crossed the Lochar again, only to frighten a couple of rustics who were pulling thistles at Cockpool. A horse seemingly bolted and did not stop till it reached the English side of the Solway. A fisherman hid in the woods all night and told his family the next day he had come across 'a bogle with long horns, eyes like trenchers and a back like a hedgehog'. He died of tuberculosis shortly afterwards.

There was no talk of the 'grumphie' during the year 1987 in Ruthwell but there was plenty else to chatter about. One person who will testify to this is Robert Nicol, the twenty-fifth minister of the parish since the Reformation. For, during the year he not only said grace before the Queen: he conducted a centenary service for the restoration of the renowned Ruthwell Cross.

On 1 November, the kirk (the oldest in southern Scotland to be used continuously as a church), was packed to celebrate a special thanksgiving service to mark the centenary of the cross's return from the wilderness. One of Scotland's leading religious

Ruthwell Cross, side detail *(Courtesy: Dumfries and Galloway Tourist Board)*

historians, the Revd Professor Alec Cheyne, Professor Emeritus of Church History at Edinburgh University, was there.

The cross, a sermon on stone which speaks of the life and passion of Christ in its carvings, carries the oldest existing piece of written English and dates back to around 680 AD. It is a priceless work of art. Yet if the General Assembly of the Church of Scotland had had its way, it would have been destroyed. For in 1640, in post-Reformation zeal, the Assembly passed the Act anent Idolatrous Monuments which outlawed 'images of popery'.

The Ruthwell Cross had survived the pillagings of the Danish sea-rovers, but now it was being reduced to the status of an unwanted totem pole, and was being threatened by Christians. It was the oldest cross of its kind in the British Isles and owed its origin to the Celtic church of Columba and not to the teachings of Rome, but the Assembly thought it reeked of Catholicism.

Thanks to a succession of forward-thinking ministers, the Cross survived. The Revd Gavin Young, minister at Ruthwell from 1617 to 1671, carried out the letter of the law by digging a trench in the kirk's clay floor and laying the cross down in three equal parts. There the precious monument lay – providing an impromptu seat for the congregations for a century and a half – until it was thrown outside to make way for renovations. Along came the Revd Henry Duncan, who not only founded the world's first savings bank, but also reconstructed the cross. First he erected it in a corner of the churchyard, and then he had it put up in his glebe.

The next threat to the runic cross with the oldest fragment of English literature came from the antiquarians of Edinburgh, who wanted it shifted to the capital. James McFarlan, Ruthwell's minister from 1871 to 1889, would have none of it; and he spearheaded the moving of it back into the kirk, one of whose sides had to be knocked down to accommodate it. It was a long and costly process, and on 21 October 1887, when the rededication of the cross was only ten days away, the Revd McFarlan wrote: 'This is one of the loveliest days of the year. Nature, still and silent, is slowly dying in her gold and red, and with the softest sunlight tending her demise. Would that this had been the day for the re-opening of my old kirk; but it is

Revd Dr Henry Duncan, Father of Savings Banks *(From the Savings Banks Museum, London)*

the day when at last I see definitely the end to this long and lonely business.'

On 31 October, according to MacFarlan's wife, the face of Moses as he descended from the Mount could not have shone more brightly than that of her husband.

Thanks to Messrs Young, Duncan and McFarlan, the Ruthwell church visitors' book of the late twentieth century has a cosmopolitan flavour: a random glance at it reveals signatures from Canada, Denmark, Portugal, France and the Philippines. It is an integral part of the Solway Heritage Trail which runs along the coast from Annan to Whithorn in Galloway, the site of Scotland's oldest church. During the cross's many years in the wilderness, one of the cross-beams went missing, but the Revd Nicol tells me: 'I live in hope that some day I'll pop into somebody's byre and see it above a door used as a lintel.'

Another well-known attraction in the village of Ruthwell is the Savings Bank Museum in memory of the aforesaid Henry Duncan. Duncan was an amazingly talented man whose preaching of the habit of thrift led to the establishment in 1810 of the Ruthwell Parish Bank, the world's first bank based on proper business principles. He was a noted philanthropist, and imported a cargo of corn from Liverpool which was dished out to the starving parishioners at considerable personal loss.

Duncan also founded an early 'Dad's Army', the Ruthwell Volunteers, as a bulwark against Napoleon. And he was founder of both the *Dumfries Standard* and the *Dumfries Courier* newspapers. There's more: he was a noted naturalist, archaeologist, novelist, economist, philosopher and landscape gardener.

Duncan was also the first man to find reptilian fossil footprints in the sandstone on Corncockle Moor near Templand.

Many people visited Duncan's manse, where he was often to be seen with a spade in the hand. A contemporary described his glebe as 'a little Eden in a world of sin'. And when an old-fashioned Secessionist minister from Dumfries visited one balmy June day and met Mrs Duncan at the gate, he is said to have remarked, 'Mam, when ye dee and gang tae heaven, ye'll think ye have never been oot o't.'

After the Disruption, Duncan became minister of the Free Church of Mount Kedar where an obelisk was erected in his memory. His statue outside the Trustees Savings Bank in Dumfries, known locally as 'The Stane Man', was the first statue erected in a public place in the town. Ruthwell museum, however, is the finest memorial to the man – which reminds me: Robert Nicol said grace before the Queen in 1987 during the opening of the new TSB headquarters in Edinburgh. They called it Henry Duncan House.

As a boy, Duncan met Robert Burns at his father's manse at Lochrutton a few miles west of Dumfries. Burns himself was a regular visitor to Ruthwell manse during his last-ditch attempt to find a cure for his terminal illness by dipping in the Solway Firth. At the time it was occupied by Duncan's predecessor, John Craig, whose daughter Agnes became Duncan's first wife.

In the course of one visit to Ruthwell manse for tea, Agnes rose to draw the blinds in order to prevent the sun from dazzling the poet. But the dying bard told her, prophetically: 'Let the sun shine in upon us, my dear young lady; he has not now long to shine for me.' The manse where this dramatic incident took place no longer exists, but a new manse was built on its site in 1890. It is now the Kirklands Hotel.

Burns had resorted to the Brow Well on the Solway, thinking it might rid him of the rheumatic heart disease he had contracted as a youngster. According to one of his biographers, Catherine Carswell, 'he waded shakily – he had to wade a long way to get to the required depth – into the chill Atlantic water, that he might stand obediently up to his armpits till it was time to drag his aching joints out again and slowly dry himself and sip his allowance of port'.

Burns also might have tramped a few 'shite-flukes' or flounders for his supper when he was there. It is an old custom which dies hard; in fact in Palnackie on the Galloway side of the firth, the world flounder tramping championships are held every July. (In harder times I have had a fridge full of flukes).

Burns drank from the well at the Brow, despite a warning from the Revd Craig that when the water was mixed with brandy it changed to an inky colour, and a florin dropped in it quickly covered in 'black varnish'.

Ruthwell also used to have its salt-panners. Along the creeks at Priestside merse (the original site of the Ruthwell Cross), if you look hard enough you can see the remains of the salt-pits which closed early last century when the salt-tax was abolished. After the Restoration, Ruthwell salters had successfully petitioned Parliament for exemption from a salt-tax levied by Cromwell. A tax was introduced later but the salters remained exempt because their product was noted for its purity. Tradition has it that James VI granted the inhabitants the unique privilege of manufacturing salt duty-free after passing through the area; so impressed was he with their industriousness.

Coal-mining might have become as important an industry at Ruthwell as it was in Whitehaven but, as the Revd Craig put it in his contribution to the *Statistical Account of Scotland (1792):* 'The want of success in this research upon the Scotch side may proceed from an inefficacy of the trials and probably the unskilfulness and knavery of those employed in making them.'

It should be mentioned here that when the travel writer, Richard Ayton, passed through at the beginning of last century, he was bewildered by the mud huts of the people of Powhellin near the Brow. He found the natives very intelligent. Every single house possessed a book, and nobody was illiterate. However, he observed that 'though they were distinguished above the poor of any other country for their mental cultivation they are in their domestic habits as uninformed as Hottentots'.

Tony Ptolomey, the laird of Comlongon Castle, is certainly no Hottentot. In fact he has turned his fifteenth century keep near Clarencefield into a country hotel and popular weekend retreat. The castle has even been mentioned in a book called *The Lovers' Guide to Britain.*

Tony, (who thinks he is descended from the first geographer to map Scotland), bought the castle in 1979, and spent several years renovating it. He chauffeurs couples to and from Gretna by Rolls Royce to get married. They have a champagne toast in the back of the Rolls before being whisked to Gretna Green for an anvil wedding, and then back to Comlongon for a candlelit dinner and a tour of the dungeons. Bridge weekends, 'murder' weekends and weekends devoted to Trivial Pursuits were all on the cards when I spoke to Tony – as were medieval nights and Burns recitation nights, with a translator on stand-by for those unfamiliar with the Scots vernacular.

Tony and his wife Brenda live in the adjacent Edwardian mansion. They have dredged a swamp and turned it into a popular trout loch. Perhaps the top attraction at Comlongon is their alleged ghost, 'the green lady', (Lady Marion Carruthers) who seemingly threw herself from the battlements rather than marry the then Duke of Buccleuch's nephew, John McMath.

Caerlaverock Castle *(Drawing: Ian A Rogers)*

Marion is immortalised in a haunting ballad.

Another castle in the immediate area attracts far more custom than Comlongon. Caerlaverock, the former stronghold of the wardens of the Western Marches, is the most visited castle in Dumfries and Galloway, and in 1988, a total of 25 992 marvelled at its ruins. The castle, built in 1220, must have witnessed some dramatic moments in history and seen the fluctuating fortunes of the Scots and the English. It was besieged and captured by Edward I and his 3000-strong army in 1300. Cromwell took it in 1651, and the Covenanters also laid siege. Sir William Wallace rested there before routing the last remnants of an English force near Cockpool in 1297. The castle fell into disrepair from the 1660s onwards when the Maxwells of Nithsdale moved to the square tower near the church.

Some historians think King Arthur was born at Caerlaverock and that the name is a corruption of *Caer Lewarch Og,* the fortess of Lewarch the Younger.

A mile or so away from the proud fortress is a tourist attraction of a different nature: a National Nature Reserve (NNR) run by the Nature Conservancy Council (NCC). Until 1957 Caerlaverock Merse was one of the largest unreclaimed salt marshes in Britain. That year it became Scotland's first

Feeding time at Eastpark Wildfowl Refuge, Caerlaverock *(Courtesy: Dumfriesshire Newspaper Group)*

national wildfowl refuge, and Britain's third. It was the first reserve in Britain to allow shooting and conservation to run hand in hand. Shooting, however, is only allowed on a certain section of the reserve and only by permit.

The establishment of the NNR on 14 000 acres of the Duke of Norfolk's land brought an end to the shooting free-for-all that had existed, and it began to bump up the numbers of the rare Spitsbergen barnacle geese (which Dumfries and Galloway Regional Council adopted as their logo in 1989). During the Second World War the Solway salt merses had been used for bombing practice, and the tanks scared the geese away so that only 400 were left in 1957. Each year now there is a record number from the frozen north. At the last count there were nearly 11,000 – the whole of the Spitsbergen group.

The Wildfowl Trust run their refuge within the reserve on 800 acres of merse and 470 acres of farmland at Eastpark Farm. The late Sir Peter Scott, the naturalist, visited regularly. Princess Alexandra opened a bird-hide there in 1988 – a typical example of the Trust's oft-criticised commercialism.

If you visit Eastpark Farm, and it is an ideal place to take children and 'adopt a duck', you'll see a wealth of birdlife wintering on the merses. There are hides in the hawthorn hedges and there are watchtowers. You'll see Bewick's swans, whoopers, pinkfeet, greylags and a host of feathered rarities. If you are peel-eyed you may see a peregrine falcon, a short-eared owl or a hen harrier.

The refuge, which was set up in 1970, is also home to Britain's most northerly colony of Natterjack toads. Appealing little creatures whose existence is threatened by industrial development and land drainage, they are, nevertheless, protected by the law: it is an offence even to photograph them without a permit from the NCC.

In the dry summer of 1987, a local farmer, John Graham, saved hundreds of Natterjack tadpoles by carting 5000 gallons of water in his slurry-tank to their ponds to stop them drying out. Others have shown themselves to be conservation-conscious, too . . . even the ICI. The projected closure of the explosives factory run by the conglomerate at Powfoot came as a bitter blow to the 127 workers but the good news for the Natterjacks was that they had squatters' rights. Conservationists croaked with delight when 1000 baby toads were born in the factory ponds in 1988. The management stepped in to excavate new ponds when the old ones were overgrown.

May is the time to be on the Solway coast to hear the evocative cry of the male Natterjack. His chorus is a familiar one both to local folk and to the security guards at the factory. For the record it goes something like this: rrrrRUP, rrrrrrRUP, rrrrrRUP!

SECTION 3: *MID ANNANDALE*

CHAPTER 9

The Tragedy of Lockerbie

Before evil terrorists catapulted my home town into the world's headlines it was a quiet little market town, a rural backwater whose main claims to historical note were the battle of Dryfe Sands which was fought in 1593, and Scotland's largest and last lamb fair, held on a local hillside for centuries.

Percy Toplis, the 'Monocled Mutineer', spent a night in the police cells in Lockerbie in 1911 after his arrest in connection with the theft of railway tickets at Annan. There was a flurry of press activity in 1978 as reporters retraced the footsteps of the 'Monster Butler', Archibald Hall, who had lived a few miles east of Lockerbie, and again following two bank robberies in the 1980s.

Before 21 December 1988, 'Black Wednesday', Lockerbie was a comparatively obscure little place – to many only a name on a signpost along the A74 dual carriageway. During the Blackpool illuminations, police had had to timetable the hundreds of buses which clogged the town on their way south, but that was before the arterial A74 by-passed the town, and before motorway service stations reduced its strategic importance. Long before Black Wednesday, Lockerbie had become a dormitory town. But since then many column miles of newspapers have been devoted to the place.

Wednesday, 21 December 1988, was arguably the most tragic day in Dumfriesshire's history. It cancelled Christmas in Lockerbie and generated the town's most melancholy New Year. All the world knows now of Britain's worst air disaster, when a Pan Am Jumbo Jet exploded over Dumfriesshire on its way to the United States, killing all 258 passengers. Thankfully (although numbers mean nothing to the bereaved) only eleven local people lost their lives when a large part of the jet gouged a monstrous crater in a, hitherto, tranquil crescent on the outskirts of town.

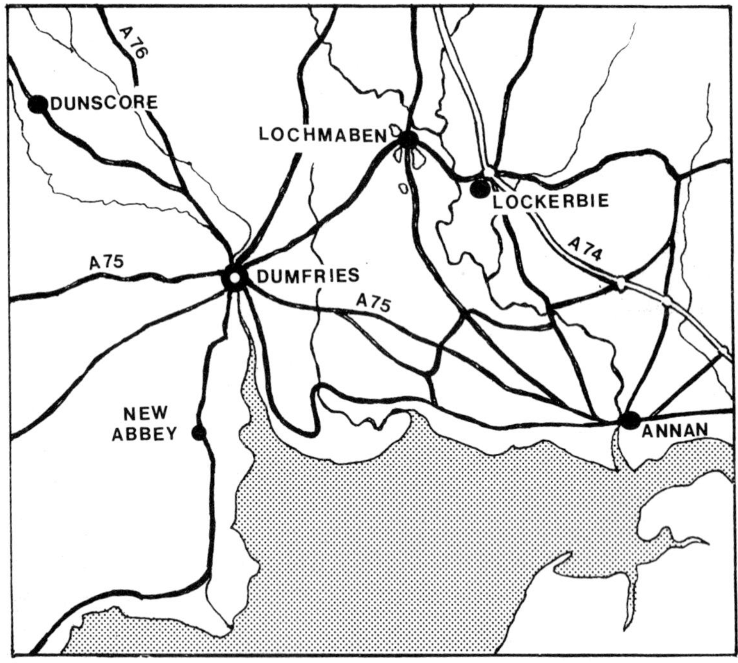

Map drawn by Ian A Rogers

The shortest day of any year is 21 December but for rescuers at Lockerbie it was the longest night. Chaos reigned and motorists caused traffic jams trying to get in to see if their relatives were okay. Many wept at the sight of the carnage that night, and I was one of them. As houses blazed in Sherwood Crescent, I remembered stealing apples in their gardens as a boy. It had been a quiet loop of residential houses favoured by retired people. As helicopters hovered above the golf-course with searchlights looking for corpses that frightful night, I remembered bashing a worn golf ball about it as a nipper with a putter discarded by a more affluent relative.

As I gazed at the Jumbo's compacted nose section which had twisted out of the sky and landed in a field near Tundergarth, I thought of happier days when I had cycled past with a badminton racquet strapped to my back. My old school, too, was transformed beyond recall, into a communications centre.

Floral tribute at Lockerbie *(Courtesy: Dumfries and Galloway Standard)*

The ice rink, in normal times one of the busiest in Scotland and the venue of international curling, was requisitioned as a mortuary. And the town hall which had been the seat of local government until reorganisation in 1974, and which normally held nativity plays and dog shows, was a chapel of rest. Work on the town hall had begun exactly a century before the jet crash, to mark Queen Victoria's jubilee. It was all terribly bizarre.

Sixteen months before the tragedy I had interviewed Davie Edwards in his Sherwood Crescent home. He was into his second kidney transplant and had won three medals at the British Transplant Olympics. Christmas 1988 saw him homeless, but alive. He had been in his garden shed fixing a puncture. His house was gutted. Fortunately, his wife and two sons were out at the time.

One of my friends, Bob Mitchell, had been walking along Rosebank Crescent when he was blown into a garden by the explosion. 'It was like a juggernaut flying through the sky,' he told me. 'It hit a house. When I came to, a body fell in front of me. It had a Pan Am badge on. I never want to see anything like that again, even in a nightmare.'

Hogmanay 1988 saw Lockerbie eerily quiet. Over the road from the 'Cross' a sad message was pinned to a bouquet of flowers. It was from a man called Chas who had travelled only the first leg of the flight, from Frankfurt to London. He had written: 'To the little girl in the red dress who lies here, who made my flight from Frankfurt such fun. You didn't deserve this. God bless.'

In normal times, and I hope my home town gets back to normal, Lockerbie is an attractive base for tourists who want to explore Annandale's varied charms. An archetypal agricultural community, it sits huddled beneath smooth hills, has a busy 'west coast line' railway station, and is the first main stop-over town off the A74 north of the border. There are many burns and rivers nearby. There are lochs and enchanting views of rich pastureland – a dominant feature of the surrounding landscape.

Current proposals for the upgrading of the A74 to motorway status are expected to have a detrimental effect on the town (population around 4000) whose employment opportunities are already fairly limited: Lockerbie has no major employer, save the academy – the only place with more than a hundred employees. Preferential treatment given to Lockerbie by the authorities after the tragedy is expected to counter-balance any problems faced by a new motorway.

Hoteliers, meanwhile, are lucky to have the dual carriageway nearby, and nearly a quarter of the population are employed in distribution and hotels.

It was the woollen industry and Lockerbie's strategic position during coaching days that transmogrified it from a hamlet of hovels built of 'shite and stanes' to a prosperous community with neat thatched cottages and, reportedly, benevolent landlords.

Lockerbie's biggest day of the year for many generations until it stopped in 1869 was the Lamb Fair at which up to 70 000 beasts changed hands. Everybody from within a twelve-mile radius of the town packed Lockerbie for the August gathering, they say. When farm servants and other workers engaged with an employer, they saw to it beforehand that they were to have Dryfesdale Sacrament Day and the Lockerbie Lamb Fair as their two holidays of the year.

Thomas Henderson, a local solicitor in the 1930s, wrote that he could remember not being able to get from the King's Arms Hotel to the Crown because of the huge crowds thronging the various markets on fair day. He painted a vivid scene in his book, *Lockerbie, A Narrative of Bygone Days.*

> 'The street was thronged from morning till late at night with merry lads and lasses clad in holiday attire, and with more matured and sedate folks, old soldiers with wooden legs and musicians in faded cloth playing the fiddle, the melodeon and the flute,' he wrote.
>
> 'On the village green were stalls laden with crockery, snaps, gingerbread, snuff, lace, buttons, pipes, tobacco, tinder-boxes, candle-moulds and cottons, and many other articles; there were also quacks, mountebancks, fat women and dwarfs, competitions at wrestling, climbing the greasy pole, sack races and hunting pigs with soapy tails; also mimic operas, men swallowing fire, and pedlars giving away their goods for nothing in order to attract the crowd and telling truths mixed with lies, and many other shows and amusements.'

At night the noisy revellers made the rafters of the inns shake with merriment: this was the only day of the year many saw their old acquaintances. It was reunion day. The Revd William McDougall was another writer who recorded his memories of the big day. And he painted an equally colourful picture of the Lockerbie races which took place the following day. The races were eventually banned by magistrates because of the civil disorder caused by the demon drink. The minister wrote of 'riot, wassail, fisticuffs and sweethearting; to be

Dumfriesshire Hunt Point-to-point at Lockerbie *(Courtesy: Dumfriesshire Newspaper Group)*

finished up in the town in the gloaming or continued in the public house to the wee short hour beyond the twal'.

He added: 'The vicious or incapable were left to their own sweet will on the hill among the quick dispersing stands and tents, or to lie in the shelter of some wood or bank to sleep off their debauch, and rise with the larks in the morning.'

Racing at Lockerbie is now confined to the annual point-to-point organised by the Dumfriesshire Hunt and run at Roberthill, a couple of miles west of the town on the road to Dumfries. At the races, in April, ordinary punters mingle with shooting-stick-toting gentry who have bars in the backs of their Volvos or four-tracks, and are proud of Dumfriesshire being a heartland of fox-hunting.

The Dumfriesshire pack, based at Kettleholm on Sir Rupert Buchanan-Jardine's Castlemilk estate, was established in 1848 with Lord Drumlanrig as master and Joe Graham as the huntsman. So revered was Joe that, when he died, an obelisk was erected in his memory on Almagill Hill near Dalton.

Otter-hunting used to be popular too – until conservationists succeeded in getting it outlawed. The delightful beasts are scarcely to be seen along the banks of the county's rivers now, although a guidebook of the 1950s stated that they were fairly plentiful. Now the Kettleholm otterhounds (established in 1889) hunt for mink instead. Incidentally, proponents of bloodsports, who argue that the hounds never killed very many otters, should read the profile of the late Mr David Bell-Irving, who bragged of possessing a staff bearing 399 notches. Each recorded the death of an otter!

A glance at the local telephone directory will yield the names of many Johnstones and Jardines, whose ancestors did hunting of a different kind. They hunted Maxwells. Indeed the Johnstones and Jardines were continually at war with their rivals from Nithsdale. The battle of Dryfe Sands was the climax of the vendetta between the families. Lord Maxwell had gathered 2000 men and marched into Annandale to besiege the laird Johnstone's house at Lochwood. To cut a long story short, the Maxwells were totally routed and lost 700 men. Many of them drowned in Gotterby Ford, and lots more went home shaken and bearing gashes made fashionable more recently by city gangs. The gash became known as 'a Lockerbie Lick'. Another interpretation of the phrase, A Lockerbie Lick, is the cracking of a nut with a sledgehammer. And that's what the Johnstones did. They even burned down the old Lochmaben church to try to smoke the Maxwells out of hiding. A few years after the battle, Sir James Johnstone met with Lord Maxwell, and the latter killed him on a spot near Tinwald, which became known as Murder Loch. There is a memorial stone to Sir James in Johnstone Parish Church.

If you wander up Lockerbie High Street and cast your eye towards the town hall you'll see the Old Tower across the road at the junction of Station Square and Bridge Street. It is the town's oldest building. Though it now houses a chip shop, it was the location where many years ago another prominent Johnstone pretended to surrender to Lord Maxwell and ended up braining him with a heavy key.

Another anecdote about the Lockerbie families tells how a traveller tried to get food and shelter at hostelries in town, but was refused entry. He, apparently, shouted out loud into one of the inns: 'Are there none of you Christians?' Came the spirited reply: 'No, only Johnstones and Jardines'.

Yet another tale tells of the River Dryfe and the proverb of

Thomas the Rhymer. The minstrel warned: 'Let spades and shovels dae what they may, Dryfe will have the Dry'sdale kirk away.' Sure enough, in 1617, the Bishop of Glasgow found that the river was threatening to wash away the original church at Sandbed, and he ordered its course to be altered. It led to a fight between neighbouring landlords, one of whom was killed. In 1671, the church was removed and built on an embankment beside Dryfe Road. The river altered its course again and threatened the church. In 1757, it was rebuilt far away from the river, at the northern end of Lockerbie. The modern church of Dryfesdale was built in 1896 well within the town. I reckon it is fairly safe from the river now.

North of Lockerbie stands a quaint reminder of Thomas Telford's association with Dumfriesshire and of Lockerbie's importance on the coaching map. It is a neat little cottage which is the only surviving, unaltered example of a Telford toll-bar built early last century.

Yet another curio in the Lockerbie area stands rather incongruously in a former Prisoner of War (POW) camp on the fringe of a conifer plantation on the road to Dalton: Scotland's first Ukrainian orthodox church. Willie Chomonczack passed his homeland's 1000th anniversary of the adoption of Christianity in 1988 in his usual capacity as the church's honorary custodian. Willie is the only surviving resident of the POW camp and he stays in one of the original cells. There is a strong Ukrainian community in Dumfriesshire, so Willie feels duty-bound to look after their church. Weddings and christenings still take place there in a corrugated hut. Part of a complex once patrolled by sharp-eyed sentries, it is topped by a makeshift spire and does not look very interesting from the outside. Inside, however, it has all the trappings of a religious sanctuary.

Gone are the halcyon days of Hallmuir, when 400 prisoners had sing-songs and dances and debates. But Willie makes it clear that, as long as there's breath in his body, he will see to it that a quiet corner of rural Dumfriesshire is forever the Ukraine.

Ecclefechan, or 'the Fechan', just down the road from little Ukraine was an important coaching-stop at one time and is known the world over as the birthplace of Thomas Carlyle.

Carlyle's House at Ecclefechan

Although little read today, the 'Sage of Chelsea' was one of the greatest men of the nineteenth century. An egotistical, hero-worshipping anti-democrat and racist he may have been, but he was also a philosophical genius and visionary, noted for his *magnum opus, The French Revolution.*

Carlyle was born the son of a stonemason in 1795 and walked the hundred miles or so to Edinburgh University when he was thirteen. When he got there he became a bookworm, and obsessed with German literature he abandoned his religious vocation. His first published words were in the *Dumfries Courier* of 8 February 1814, and he later relied on commissioned freelance work to pay the bills as he rose to prominence. He suffered from indigestion, constipation and piles most of his life, which may account for his short temper with such people as Coleridge, whom he referred to as 'a round, fat, oily yet impatient little man, sunk inextricably in the depths of putrescent indolence, an inspired ass'.

Carlyle never forgot his roots, though. And when he died he was buried in the village churchyard, having refused a place among the great in the cloisters of Westminster Abbey. His birthplace, the Arched House, is in the hands of the National Trust for Scotland. The house, which was built by Telford's father, has been carefully restored and refurbished in period style: a modest shrine to a man who was one of the most influential thinkers of his generation. Many of the Sage's books and papers, and relics of the family can be seen by visitors. His parents' clock still ticks in the kitchen, while outside the burn (the Kuhbach of *Sartor Resartus*) still babbles by, as it would have done when Carlyle was a boy who wondered at the hoarse cawing of the rooks above neighbouring Woodcockair.

Carlyle's statue, given by his nephew Alexander Carlyle in 1929, still stands opposite the Haggs at the top of the village like a god overseeing his domain. He is buried alongside Archibald Arnott, who was medical attendant to Napoleon at St Helena, and had lived at Kirkconnel Hall, which is now a hotel, at the northern end of the village.

There's a story about a literary pilgrim who visited the village once in search of the Carlylean atmosphere. We are told he approached one of the locals for information. Quothe the villager: 'Tam Carlyle, aye there wis Tam! He went tae London, they tell me he wrote books. But there's his brother, Jeems – he was the mahn o' the faimily. He drove mair pigs intae Fechan mairkit than ony ither fairmer in the parish.'

Robert Burns's first taste of Ecclefechan did not endear him to it. Ten months before Carlyle was born, the bard was snowed up in the village. And he described it to a friend as an 'unfortunate, wicked little village' where a fiddler was 'torturing Catgut, in sounds that would have insulted the dying agonies of a sow under the hands of the butcher'.

Added Burns: 'I have been in a dilemma whether to get drunk and forget these miseries, or to hang myself, to get rid of them: like a prudent man (a character congenial to my every thought, word and deed) I of two evils have chosen the least, and am very drunk.'

Historians suspect Burns also got involved with the daughter of the village postmaster during his stay. In between times he won a wager for getting a word to rhyme with Ecclefechan. Here is his prize-winning entry:

Then up we raise, and took the road
An in by Ecclefechan,
Where brandy-stoup we gart it clink,
And the strang beer ream the quech in.

There are many places of historical importance within striking distance of Ecclefechan. Hoddom Castle is one of them. It is being promoted by a Southampton-based company in 1989 as the centre of a £40 million leisure complex, the like of which Dumfriesshire has never seen. Plans include two championship golf courses, a five-star hotel (on the site of the castle), an equestrian centre and a luxury holiday village catering for shooting, hunting, fishing and golfing packages. There is talk of both Steve Ovett and Tony Jacklin getting involved. Ovett owns Kinmount mansion near Annan.

Above the castle (which incidentally was the venue of the first Scottish experiment in artificial insemination), stands Repentance Tower, a lone sentinel on Beacon Hill. From the tower there can be few finer views in southern Scotland: on a clear day you can see the Isle of Man, the Lakeland peaks, the Moffat and Lowther hills, the Ae Forest and the gleaming Solway Firth.

The tower was a watchtower in a chain of defence posts in the front line against the Auld Enemy. Many a tale is told about its origin, the most generally accepted of which is as follows: Sir John Maxwell, whose family had been wardens of the Western Marches and Hereditary Stewards of Annandale for centuries, was one of the 'assured Scots' whom the English had under their thumbs. In February 1548 Lord Wharton the English warden mounted an offensive and reached as far north as Durisdeer to confront the Douglases. On the eve of the battle however, Maxwell, a powerful figure in Scottish affairs, was bribed to switch sides, in return for the hand of Agnes Herries and a rich dowry.

Consequently, Wharton retreated to Carlisle. Maxwell became Lord Herries and Warden of Caerlaverock. His treachery, however, cost the lives of twelve of his kinsmen who had been held by authority of Henry VIII as hostages at Carlisle castle. One of them was his twelve-year-old nephew.

Maxwell apparently built the tower as a symbol of his remorse. Some folk say, though, that it is called Repentance Tower because Herries built Hoddom Castle out of stones from Trailtrow chapel, and later thought better of it. Yet another legend has Herries cutting prisoners' throats and throwing them overboard while he was returning from

Steve Ovett at Kinmount Mansion, near Annan *(Courtesy: Dumfriesshire Newspaper Group)*

Repentance Tower, vantage point extraordinaire

England with a boatload of booty.

On the other side of the River Annan, beneath the wooded hill of Woodcockair where James IV once hunted, is the old churchyard of St Kentigern – said to be the site of an eighth century abbey, an eleventh century graveyard and a medieval church. The saint set up a cathedral on the present site of Glasgow, but ten years later fled the pagan Britons. He returned to Scotland when Rhydderech ap Tudwell became king of Strathclyde, and settled at Hoddom. There he remained until it was safe to return to what would become Glasgow. He was known there as 'Mungo' or dear friend.

Long before the day of Kentigern the Romans made their mark on Dumfriesshire, and one of their forts was on Burnswark Hill. The hill is unusually flat-topped and is visible from a great distance. Its use as a defensive site is – like Repentance Tower's – obvious from the panoramic views. The hill is accessible by taking the road to Middlebie for half a mile and branching off to the left.

CHAPTER 10

Marjorie o' the Monie Lochs

Fittingly did writers of Burns's day compare Lochmaben to a Venice rising out of the water, and the poet himself had good reason to christen this appealing town 'Marjorie o' the Monie Lochs'. Let's face it: there can be very few other settlements in the world with nine lochs around them.

Since Burns's time, the Grummel Loch, once used for ducking witches, has been drained and in-filled with rubbish. And Halleaths or Broomhill Loch has been drained and plastered with conifers. That leaves the Castle Loch, the Kirk Loch, the Mill Loch, the Hightae Loch, Upper Loch and the two 'Blind Lochs'.

In the days of hard winters, the Castle Loch was a curler's paradise; it is now a centre for yachtsmen, and along with the Mill Loch it provides some of the best coarse fishing in Dumfries and Galloway.

Lochmaben lochs have something else to trumpet, however. The Castle and Mill Lochs were the only habitats in the world of the vendace, a freshwater fish shrouded in mystique and prized for its flesh. Local romance has it that Mary, Queen of Scots introduced it. Or was it Robert the Bruce or an arcane order of Italian monks? Scientists scotch the myths and say *Coregonus vandesius* swam into the area thousands of years ago and was land-locked by the ice age.

What is beyond doubt is the fact that vendace were for gourmets. One wrote: 'A dinner or supper of vendace, with other combinations of fish or fowl, is a feast for gods and men. They melt in the mouth as a sweet, and a wee drappie from the town cellars to wash it down is the height of gastronomic pleasure.'

The dish was not to everybody's taste, though. Legend has it that King James VI was offered vendace at a banquet in his honour in Dumfries in 1617. Seemingly, they had been chosen by the chef with an assurance that they were a local delicacy which would prove favourable to the royal palate. 'James, thinking they emitted a peculiar smell and had an inauspicous

Chilly dusk on the Castle Loch, Lochmaben, sole habitat of the vendace *(Courtesy: Dumfriesshire Newspaper Group)*

appearance, viewed them with almost as much horror as was felt by his ancestor Macbeth when the ghost of Banquo glided in to disturb the feast at Glamis,' wrote the historian McDowall in his *History of Dumfries*.

'Starting to his feet, he shouted, "Treason", and it was not until the offending dish was removed that he resumed his seat and his equanimity.'

The Dumfriesshire aristocracy adored vendace, even if the king did not. They even formed an exclusive club to fish for them. Provost Robert Fraser wrote in the 1950s: 'It is recorded by a county lady who was present in the late 1860s that the Maxwell family arrived from Terregles House in a boat of their own mounted on wheels and drawn by four horses ridden by postilions; the wheels were removed and the boat was launched.

'When sufficient fish were caught, the catch was sent to the inn selected as the club headquarters for the day – and cooked according to a time-honoured formula that was a closely guarded secret.'

Later a more democratic club was founded, and the vendace fishing became a public holiday. But all good things must pass: the last fishing took place on the Mill Loch in 1912, and the catch was small. Over forty years later, Dr Peter Maitland, a world expert on freshwater fish, warned that adequate steps would have to be taken to stop the vendace from becoming extinct. His prophecy was fulfilled. The Nature Conservancy Council took until March 1988 to protect the species.

'I'm glad something's been done, but it's a pity action wasn't taken decades ago. The Lochmaben Vendace is almost certainly extinct now,' said Dr Maitland, a month or so later.

The NCC acted slightly more quickly with the Mill Loch. They declared it a Site of Special Scientific Interest – twenty years after the zoologist's warning that its inhabitants would soon die out.

The only vendace left are those in private collections – stuffed ones. One can be viewed in a glass case in the town hall.

Lochmaben is famous as the former seat of Robert the Bruce's family, although the last remnants of their first castle, the motte, is now the fourteenth tee on the town's golf course (there is some evidence that an Iron Age shrine to the god Mapros stood there). The present Lochmaben Castle stands in glorious ruins at the southern end of the Castle Loch (the peninsula on which it stands was an island at one time, but the water level was lowered by dredging the outlet burn). An early fourteenth century bell called the Bruce Bell is still used in Lochmaben church.

The fortress saw its share of history. It was the scene of the abortive Albany Raid in 1484, the first step in an attempted coup by the Duke of Albany. Later, in 1774, it was the meeting place for Jacobite conspirators, but the projected eleventh-hour rebellion fizzled out because of lack of support.

Eventually the castle fell into disrepair and local people plundered its stones to build dykes and walls.

Robert the Bruce's association with Lochmaben has its legacy in the twentieth century. The King's 'Kindly Tenants' are the sole survivors in Scotland of an ancient form of land tenure. They hold their land direct from the crown with the theory that the monarch never dies. And the House of Lords has rejected attempts by landowners to usurp the tenants' privileges.

Bruce originally awarded those who had served him well at Lochmaben Castle, parcels of land to be held in perpetuity. Although he did not confer a similar honour on those who had helped him at Bannockburn, he honoured his menials at the castle. And today, the residents of Greenhill, Heck, Hightae and Smallholm (the Royal Four Towns) enjoy perks like free fishing on a profitable stretch of the river Annan. The Royal Four Towns Commissioners lease out the fishing and the profits are ploughed back into a remarkably thriving community (the school must, for example, be one of the best equipped in Dumfriesshire). Kindly Tenants sell their houses to aspiring Kindly Tenants or hand the privileges down to their offspring.

Robert Burns also had strong connections with Lochmaben. A frequent visitor to and Freeman of the town, he wrote of it fondly as 'a city containing upwards of fourscore living souls that cannot discern between their right hand or left – for drunkenness has, at present, the balance of power in their hands'. The bard also described the then Provost Robert Maxwell as 'one of the soundest-headed, best-hearted whisky-drinking fellows in the south of Scotland'.

In a letter to Mrs Dunlop, Burns wrote of 200 miners from Upper Nithsdale converging on Lochmaben, meaning business in an electoral skirmish. He wrote: '. . . but when they appeared over a hilltop within a half a mile of Lochmaben, they found such a superior force of Annandale warriors drawn out to dispute the day that, without striking a stroke, they turned their backs and fled with all the precipitation the horrors of blood and murther could inspire.'

Burns often visited the minister Andrew Jaffray at his manse, now Magdalene House, in Bruce Street, and Jaffray's daughter Jean was the original of *The Blue-Eyed Lassie*.

Another famous man associated with Lochmaben was the founder of the Bank of England and the projector of the ill-fated Darien Scheme, William Paterson, who was born at Skipmyre farm, which is between Lochmaben and Torthorwald.

Paterson's nephew James Mounsey, who was also born at Skipmyre, became chief physician to Empress Elizabeth of Russia, but returned to Scotland in the reign of Catherine the Great after the murder of Tsar Peter III – reportedly to avoid the repercussions of having been privy to the scandals of the Russian court. Connoisseurs of country wines and tarts may be surprised to learn that Mounsey was the first person in Britain to plant rhubarb. He brought seeds with him from Russia and planted them in the Old Physic Garden in Edinburgh: and he gained a gold medal for his enterprise.

Mounsey, who is commemorated in Mounsey's Wynd, Lochmaben, built Rammerscales House, an imposing baronial mansion near Lochmaben, whose many doors were once thought to have been installed as 'rabbit-holes'. Mounsey, you see, was paranoid about the possibility of Russian assassins coming to Annandale to get him. There was also talk of an underground passage out of the house.

Since the eighteenth century Rammerscales has been in the hands of the Bell-Macdonald family who have links with Flora Macdonald.

As for Mounsey, he died in Edinburgh in 1773 and is buried in Lochmaben's old churchyard, which is reached by a lane next to the post office.

Beside Mounsey's obelisk there is one in memory of William Jardine, a ship's surgeon who had been born at Broadholm Farm, and became 'the greatest of the opium runners'. He was a co-founder of the Oriental combine, Jardine Matheson and Co. Jardine (1784-1843) played a crucial part in the establishment of Hong Kong. In fact his life-story was the basis of the plot of James Clavell's best seller, *Tai Pan.* Today he would be upheld as a symbol of Thatcherism – the wee country lad who played a prominent role in the expansion of the British Empire, and whose ruthless entrepreneurial style made him a very wealthy man.

However, largely thanks to Jardine's enterprise, opium was wasting four million addicts in China in 1833. A civil servant of the period wrote: 'The officers, scholars and people, soldiers and servants, the women and girls are all involved in this vice. Six-tenths of the people in the villages, and eight-tenths in the cities are infected by it. They look like ghosts.'

Jardine and Matheson were the top drug dealers in what was at the time the largest commerce of its type in the world. They scored in India and disposed of it in Canton. Were they operating today, they would be caged for life by the narcotics squad. When the mandarin Lin Tse-hsu vigorously halted the opium trade, however, the British Government, sent in the military. The reason: to avoid a recession. Sixteen men-of-war,

Dr William Jardine *(Courtesy: Jardine Matheson & Co Ltd)*

four armed steamers and 4000 soldiers annihilated the Chinese armada. The British got Hong Kong, the equivalent of £30 million in Mexican dollars, and of course trade re-opened in Canton. The First Opium War had been won.

Benjamin Disraeli called Jardine 'a dreadful man! A Scotchman, richer than Croesus, one Mr Druggy, fresh from Canton with a million in opium in each pocket, denouncing corruption and bellowing free trade'.

Many of Jardine's relatives settled in Dumfriesshire, and indeed so many heads of Jardine Matheson retired here that it was once known as Chinatown. Jardine had built up a massive

Spedlins Tower, haunted by Dunty Porteous *(Drawing: Ian A Rogers)*

business empire at the expense of many lives, and he was the man behind one of the least defensible wars in which the British were ever involved.

Still on the Jardines: one of their strongholds, Spedlins Tower, has a grizzly legend to it. 'Dunty' Porteous died in the dungeon there after gnawing off his hand in a fruitless attempt to stave off hunger. His gaoler, Sir Alexander Jardine, had gone off to Edinburgh forgetting about him. According to Grose in his *Antiquities of Scotland:* 'The castle was terribly haunted till a chaplain of the family exorcised and confined the bogle to a pit, whence it would never come out, so long as a large Bible, which he had used on that business, remained in the castle.'

The Bible was sent to the capital in 1710 to be rebound, and it is recorded that 'Dunty' hauled the baron and his wife out of bed with his fleshless hand. The Bible, whose brass-bound box is made out of one of the old beams in the tower, was returned in a bid to appease the spirit of the miller. The Jardines sold up in the 1890s and they took the Bible with them. It is now in the hands of Sir Alec Jardine, the clan chief, who lives in the Lake District.

Despite the haunting tales, the clan made their last visit to Spedlins in 1987, as part of their biennial gathering from around the world. During the visit, the tour's coach driver was accidentally shut inside a cupboard. The door refused to budge until one of the Jardines arrived and opened it with a trowel. The knight in shining armour was a funeral director!

SECTION 4: *UPPER ANNANDALE*

CHAPTER 11

Moffat of the Magic Waters

From towering Hartfell, the reputed seat of Merlin the magician, many a hill-walker has come to realise why they call Dumfries and Galloway 'Scotland in Miniature'. The respectable Moffat range offers an eagle's eye view of the countryside that won the hearts of Burns, Barrie, Buchan, Carlyle, Scott, Hogg and MacDiarmid.

Moffat, a former spa town with one of the broadest high streets in Scotland, thrives below these hills. It is Dumfriesshire's premier tourist town: the surrounding countryside offers the southern visitor who makes a detour off the A74 his first glimpse of real Scottish scenery. The pleasant streets of the town, which has won several prizes in the Britain in Bloom competition and thrice been voted Scotland's best-kept large village, are packed in the summer months.

The town, within striking distance of Edinburgh and Glasgow, has long been the most genteel in the county, and a magnet for wealthy elderly folk, who quickly snap up what they want from the property pages and become addicts of the town's famous Moffat Toffee.

Moffat's metamorphosis from a gauche village of herds and dykers to one of Scotland's most fashionable resorts was due to the discovery of Moffat Well by minister's daughter, Rachel Whiteford, in 1633. Afterwards it became a cult town, and many well-heeled travellers came its way.

What were they after? A guidebook of 150 years ago described the sulphureous spring as follows: 'In all scrofulous and scorbutic cases, it is a powerful remedy, being seldom known to prove ineffectual when the lungs were not diseased; in the removal of bilious complaints, also, it is eminently successful, as well as creating appetite and promoting digestion; and it is an excellent specific for gravel and rheumatism; it sparkles in the glass like champagne, but it is so volatile that it can be drunk in perfection only at the fountain.'

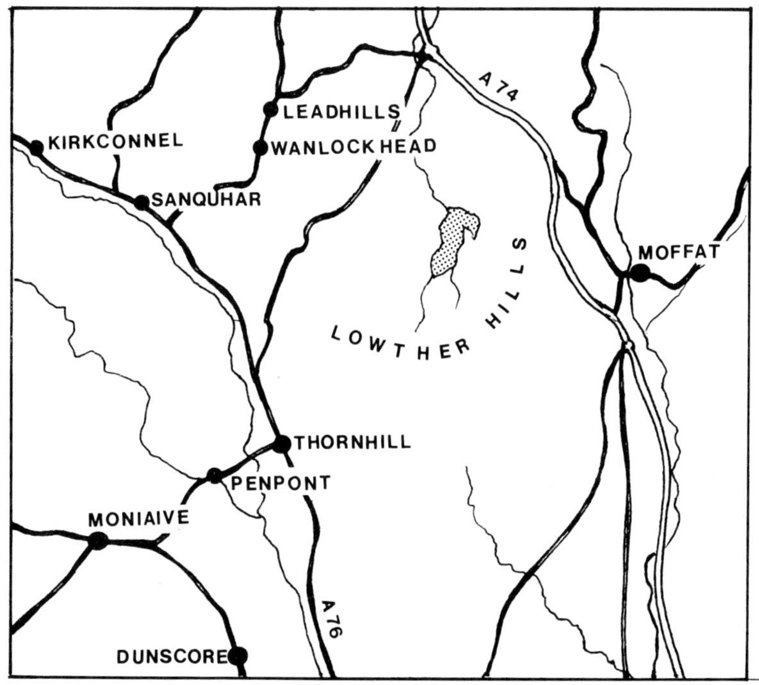

Map drawn by Ian A Rogers

For those who couldn't reach the spa there was the carry-out. After the discovery of Hartfell Spa in 1748, a local entrepreneur bottled its water and sent it all over Britain. Some bottles ended up in India and the West Indies. The Hartfell beverage – which spouted out of a rock of alum slate – was supposedly great for chest disorders. Moreover, it was beneficial in 'women's complaints' and in the 'healing of obstinate cutaneous eruptions'.

Many famous people visited the wells, including the Empress Eugenie of France. One writer commented at the end of last century: 'A sort of promenade begins every morning in summer at the very unjustifiable hour of six o'clock, and from that hour to eleven there may be seen, in that beautiful town in front of the spring, a series of visitors of all ranks, imbibing the health-giving fluid with great devotion.'

Graham's *Social Life of Scotland in the Eighteenth Century* observed: 'In spring there meet round the little wells of Moffat a throng in their gayest and brightest from society in town and country, sipping their sulphur waters and discussing their pleasant gossip ... city clergy, men of letters, country gentlemen and ladies of fashion, and the diseased and decrepit of the poorest rank, who had toilsomely travelled from far-off districts to taste the magic waters.'

Many of the nation's literati came, saw, and drank – despite misgivings from critics like one Dr Garnet who wrote in 1800 that the waters of Moffat Well had 'a strong smell resembling bilge-water or the scourings of a gun'. Another detractor was a Dr Macadam who wrote fifty-eight years later that the odour of the well reminded him of 'a slightly putrescent egg'. A further disincentive had been offered by Baron John Clerk of Penicuik in 1748, when he pointed out that local lepers bathed their sores at the well.

Leprosy did not plague the travel writer and diarist, James Boswell, but he visited Moffat in 1766, ostensibly to 'wash off a few scurvy spots which the warmer climate of Europe had brought out on my skin'. John Home, the playwright, and Robert Burns also visited the healing waters, as did Dr Blacklock the blind poet, and Hugh Blair the divine.

Moffat's development as a tourist town was nurtured by the coming of the railways last century and by the number of well-appointed hotels. The oldest hotel was, and is, the Black Bull, which was visited by our national poet. It was also the headquarters of Bloody Claverhouse during the Killing Times when Covenanters found safety in the hills. There was also the Spur Inn which became the Balmoral, and the King's Arms which is now the Annandale. The King's Arms was built in the 1760s as a staging-post, and it boasted fine clientele, including an Austrian prince. The following year, in 1815, Grand Duke Nicholas was so impressed that he paid his bill twice.

The Moffat Hydropathic was a crowd-puller in its time. A splendid building, it had 300 bedrooms which were patronised by the upper classes from around Britain. They came for the mineral waters, saunas, and to play tennis in the town which hosted the Scottish Lawn Tennis Championships. Nowadays, every August, Moffat hosts the South of Scotland Lawn Tennis Championships.

Moffat's wide High Street with two of its main features, the war memorial and clock tower *(Courtesy: Dumfriesshire Newspaper Group)*

The Hydro opened in 1878, and guidebooks reveal that in 1900 it took 24 949 visitors, who sampled Turkish baths and played croquet on the lawn or stayed indoors with the masseuses. The building became a convalescent hospital for officers during the First World War, but was back in business when hostilities stopped.

Unfortunately, the Hydro was totally destroyed by fire in 1921, and Moffat's status as a tourist town has never wholly recovered. According to an innocuous-looking paragraph in the local newspaper of the time, the Hydro was burned to the ground because Moffat fire brigade did not have a long enough hose and they had to wait for reinforcements from Gretna.

For less well-off travellers there had been the baths hall, which stood on the site of the present town hall and had mineral water piped in from the wells. To less mobile seekers of health, hot mineral baths were available – at ninety-six degrees Fahrenheit – for the princely sum of two shillings. Or they could settle for a cold bath for a shilling.

James MacPherson, the man who duped the literary world with his supposed translations of the epic poems of Ossian, is said to have devised his ruse on Moffat bowling green, which stood in the middle of the High Street and was a rendezvous for men of letters. He stayed at Moffat House for a while, before he went on to become the darling of London society with his fraudulent tales of Celtic heroes.

MacPherson had played a small part in Moffat's history – a history that is mirrored in the town's museum, which is housed in an old bakehouse opposite the church. The museum tells of clan warfare and possesses fossils of some of the earth's earliest creatures unearthed at Dobbs Linn near Moffat by Professor Charles Lapworth. There is a model motte and bailey fort typical of the form of defence of Upper Annandale people in olden times. The museum has mementoes of the railways, too. And you'll find out there that John Loudon McAdam, the famous road builder, is buried in Moffat cemetery. He spent part of his early life in the town after making a fortune in New York, and his dying wish was to 'sleep amidst the mountains of Moffat'. He had rented Dumcrieff mansion near Moffat from 1783 to 1784, a house later sold to Dr Currie, the biographer of Burns, and then to Dr John Rogerson who was court physician to Catherine the Great of Russia.

Moffat is proud of her history as a centre for the sheep industry – a history reflected in the town's annual gala ceremony and recalled by the Colvin fountain which stands on the High Street, opposite the Star Hotel, the narrowest hotel in Britain. The fountain, topped by the statue of a ram, was gifted to the town by William Colvin, a prominent local businessman. Tradition has it that the sculptor committed suicide when he realised he had sculpted the ram without any ears.

Five miles north-west of Moffat is the Devil's Beef Tub, where the Border Reivers once hid their stolen cattle and where Covenanting refugees hid from the dragoons. Sir Walter Scott wrote of 'the Tub' in *Redgauntlet*: 'It looks as if four hills were laying their heads together to shut out daylight from the black, blackguardly abyss of a hole that it is, and goes straight down from the roadside as perpendicularly as it can go, to be a heathery brae.'

Rudyard Kipling, more reverently, reckoned that it 'seemed more than any other spot to be consecrated to the old gods'.

The valley has seen its share of drama. William Wallace's

Grey Mare's Tail *(Photograph: Angus Leigh, Moffat)*

brother-in-law farmed at Corehead, and the hero himself rode out from here to take Lochmaben Castle from the English. Two postmen died in a blizzard in 1831 trying to get the mail through; their memorial stands overhead.

Yet another incident saw a Highlander called McCleran roll down the hill in his plaid to escape execution in Carlisle. And the weavers of Clydesdale found safety in the glen after the Battle of Bothwell Bridge.

Many Covenanters hid in the mists here: it was a hotbed for those who escaped the King's dragoons and held secret congregations in the wilds. According to James Hogg, shepherds were scared by what they heard at night.

'The heart of the shepherd grew chill, and his hair stood on end as he hastened home to alarm the cottage circle with a tale of horror. For besides this solemn and unearthly music, he perceived lights aroving about by night in wilds and in caverns where human things had never resided and where foot of man had never trod, and he deemed that legions of spiritual creatures had once more taken possession of his solitary dells.'

So strong was the Covenanting spirit in the Southern Upland communities, however, that as late as the beginning of this century, it is said, shepherds would kill a curlew on sight since the bird's ancestors had once betrayed the hiding places of their forebears.

A gruesome find in the Beef Tub in 1934 sparked off a nation-wide murder hunt and led to the trial and execution of Dr Buck Ruxton, an Indian surgeon who had practised in Edinburgh and then Lancaster. He had murdered his wife and maid and scattered their mutilated remains around the Moffat hills. The police found thirty grisly packages, and later found a left foot on the roadside several miles south of the town. Subsequent finds included a piece of flesh and an arm.

Despite their bloody past, the Moffat hills – with the evocative Craigmichen Scaur, Saddle Yoke and Swaate Fell – are a glorious treat to the walker. The Grey Mare's Tail is one of the best-known beauty spots in the south of Scotland. It is a fine waterfall dropping 200 feet down the northern slope of the valley of the Moffat water – there's a rare U-shaped hanging valley fashioned by glaciation.

The mountain of Hartfell (2635 feet above sea level) is said by Nikolai Tolstoy, the historian, to have been the seat of Merlin the wizard – the scene of his prophetic exile in the middle of the wood of Celyddon in the second half of the sixth century. Tolstoy cites Welsh poetry to back his theory, and claims Hartfell is 'ideally suited to have been the archaic *axis mundi,* both on account of its exceptional view and from its being at the point from which spring three great rivers flowing into the seas around the Scottish lowlands – the Tweed, the Clyde and the Annan.

Tolstoy saw Hartfell spa as Merlin's *fons Galabes,* which was sited on the skirts of a mountain. There is also Arthur's Seat in the vicinity.

Hogg and Scott used to visit Loch Skeen above the Grey Mare's Tail and marvel at the beauty, even if Merlin did not. The loch is said to have once produced the finest trout in the south of Scotland. Always ice-cold – as I found out to my cost after a midsummer ramble – it has an islet, on which eagles used to nest away from damaging shepherds' slings. The grandeur is described by Scott in *Marmion*:

> Where eagles scream from shore to shore
> Down all the rocks the torrents roar
> On the bleak waves incessant driven
> Dark mists infest the summer heaven.

If local folklore is right, the last eagle to breed in the Moffat hills was brought down by a stone propelled by a catapult wielded by one Bauldy Hairstanes.

One caveat about visiting the Moffat hills: local people have come across several unexploded bombs over the years from former war testing ranges. It worried them so much that Moffat Community Council eventually wrote to the Ministry of Defence to admonish them. The usual bland reply reassured the public. In 1988, however, a man from the Ae Village discovered a hand grenade with a metal detector. Police admitted that the finder could have been in danger. It was a Bakelite Second World War grenade – after forty years it was ready to go off at the slightest movement.

Those worried about going out for an arduous and rewarding walk in the shadow of Merlin only to have their climbing boots blown off might consider the odds before they fret too much.

Talk of the war brings us to Lord Dowding, who was born in Moffat and became the leader of the Battle of Britain. Hugh, the boy who was destined to become the Drake of the air, the Architect of Deliverance and Air Chief Marshal Lord Dowding, GCB, GCV, CMG, Commander-in-Chief of RAF Fighter Command, was born in the headmaster's bedroom at St Ninian's School in April 1882.

In 1987, Miss Irene Park, the daughter of a former town Provost, broke into her life savings and bought the school as a memorial to Dowding. A former WAAF officer, the spinster had already been instrumental in getting the annual Spitfire

Eyes upward in salute to the last of the few – a Spitfire returns to the skies over Moffat, former Air Chief Marshal Lord Dowding's birthplace *(Courtesy: The Scotsman Publications Ltd)*

and Hurricane flypasts over Moffat as a tribute to Dowding. Her gamble with St Ninian's school paid off. The Royal Air Force Association bought it from her, and after a world-wide appeal for £1 million it was renovated as a sheltered housing complex in honour of the great man, who had saved his country from a Nazi invasion.

Substantial donations came from the McRobert Trust and from King Hussein of Jordan. There were sponsored cycle rides, five-a-side football tournaments, a darts marathon and a fish-in. On Ascension Island, the RAF engineering squadron pulled a gigantic Hercules aircraft 300 yards for sponsor money.

Dowding is now honoured in the International Aerospace Hall of Fame in San Diego. However, he was treated shabbily by the top brass, and he was rescued from oblivion only after his death in 1970. It is no exaggeration to say that a modest Moffatonian played a prominent part in regaining for him his rightful niche in the history books.

Said Miss Park: 'His sister used to tell me that his roots were firmly in the Scottish borders. There was a lot of Borderer in him. He was a bonnie fechter for what he knew to be right. I am sure he would have thought Dowding House right.'

Archibald Hamilton Charteris was another man of note in the Moffat area. Born in 1835, he founded the Women's Guild against the odds. For in 1886, the year before its founding, several ministers objected to the General Assembly of the Church of Scotland, telling them: 'Woman's Guild indeed, whit nonsense, they'll no stop till they get the vote.'

Charteris not only founded the Guild, he became professor of biblical criticism at Edinburgh University, Moderator of the General Assembly and chaplain to Queen Victoria and King Edward VII.

If Charteris was a remarkable man, then so was his father. John Charteris, during his forty-eight years as dominie at Wamphray school, educated many boys who were to walk the corridors of power. He turned out ten ministers, including three Moderators; nineteen doctors; eleven teachers, some of whom were headmasters. There were also surveyors, merchants, an army general, a song writer and a host of successful businessmen. And all this was achieved by John

Revd Professor Archibald Charteris (From *Alice Maxwell DCS,* Hodder & Stoughton, 1919)

Charteris in a one-roomed school with 120 pupils of all ages at any one time.

Before we leave Upper Annandale, we must hear about Moffat's connection with the aristocratic rancher and politician, Robert Cunninghame Graham. Graham wrote a number of short stories, one of which, *Beattock for Moffat,* concerned a dying man being conveyed by train from London to Moffat in search of a cure in the rural breezes. The sick man 'dying Andra' looked out of his carriage and counted the miles to Moffat. But he never made it. He died as the train rolled into Beattock station for the spur-line. His brother Jock said: 'Weel, weel, he'll hae a braw hurl onyway in the new Moffat hearse.'

SECTION 5: *NITHSDALE*

CHAPTER 12
God's Treasure-House

Scotland's highest village sits higgledy-piggledy at the head of the majestic Mennock Pass which is arguably one of the most scenic glens south of the Highlands. At 425 metres above sea level Wanlockhead is hemmed in by the heathery slopes of the Lowther Hills. It is Dumfriesshire's most northerly outpost.

The surrounding area is something special, not least because the bowels of Mennock, which cleaves the peaks, have disgorged over seventy minerals – more than any other geological site in the British Isles. Well did it earn its name, 'God's Treasure-House in Scotland'.

In 1619, the chronicler Stephen Atkinson compared the region to Paradise, and its four burns to the rivers that flowed into the Garden of Eden. For it was the country's premier non-ferrous mining area. Its gold went into the Scottish Crown Jewels, and Scottish coins called 'bonnet pieces' were minted from neighbouring Leadhills in the 1540s.

Gold was discovered in the area during the reign of James IV. In 1502, long before the Klondyke days, a nugget of gold weighing the same as a modern-day bag of sugar was howked out of the moor. Further good finds followed before the king died at Flodden in 1513.

During the subsequent regency of Albany, a group of Germans took the lease of the gold-mines; they apparently bribed the authorities to allow them to bend the bullion laws and export heaps of gold back to the Fatherland for refinement.

When Mary, Queen of Scots, took the throne, the quest for gold quickened. Thirty-five ounces of the precious metal were used for her crown; three pounds, ten ounces were used for the king's (he'd a bigger head); and another one pound, four ounces were used to make the queen a belt.

While royalty prospered, gold-digging proved costly for some – as an unfortunate young man called George Douglas

Wanlockhead, Scotland's highest village *(Photograph: Mike Wilkinson, Sunday Times, Scotland)*

discovered in 1585 when he and an avalanche crossed paths at Shortcleugh. According to Atkinson he was 'slaine with the fall of the bray after a great weete'. They found him three days later loaded with gold. One consolation was that he received a better burial than his forefathers.

Enter Bevis Bulmer. The gold rush did more for this Yorkshireman's bank balance than anyone else's before or after. With 300 men, he worked three summers and landed £300 000 worth of gold – and silver-a-plenty. Never one to hide his light under a bushel, Bulmer chiselled the following slogan on a lintel above the door of one of his houses: 'In Wanlock, Elvan and Glengonnar, I won my riches and my honour'. Ever the charmer, he presented Queen Elizabeth with a gold porringer, and later he was knighted.

Alas Bulmer followed 'idle, veniall vices to his dying day, that were not allowable of God nor man'. He died in debt to the tune of £340, undoubtedly becoming the subject of a morality tale for the Bible-bashers of the day. His only memorial is in the name Bulmer Moss near Wanlockhead.

George Bowes was the next likely lad to venture north to the Scottish El Dorado. He struck it lucky and sealed off his works. He planned to return later, but never did. Instead he fell down a mineshaft in Cumberland and broke his neck. At least two gold-thirsty craturs can still be seen now and again in the Lowther Hills with their converted frying pans searching fruitlessly for Bowes's lode.

The aforementioned Atkinson was also a prospector, and he composed an imaginative treatise for James VI in which he talked of shipwrecked sailors delivering a prophecy in the reign of Joshua about the discovery of gold mines in Scotland. According to Atkinson, Joshua had been king of Scotland in 160 BC. And the castaways said a king would be born 'having a privy signe marke or token upon his body, the like unto none shall have, who shall reigne, rule and governe in peace, and be supreme head of the Kirke, and a prince of more Kingdom than is Scotland'.

King James was hoodwinked into thinking he would become the world's richest monarch – and he offered knighthoods to successful prospectors. In his lifetime, however, only a few ounces of gold were unearthed.

The last of the organised diggers was Dr John Hyndlie, who received a grant in 1621. But he also failed to make the mines pay, and since then no serious attempt has been made to mine gold in the Wanlockhead belt. It is now in the hands of amateurs: would-be prospectors can to this day be seen bent-backed along the tributaries of the Elvan Water with their sluice-boxes and pans. In the early summer of 1940, a retired lead-miner, John Blackwood, dug up a mass of gold-bearing quartz, which produced the biggest nugget found in Scotland for two centuries. Dug up from shingle beside the Wyngate Burn, it was as big as a pullet's egg, and its home is now the British Museum.

It was lead rather than gold which underpinned the economy of Wanlockhead. The Romans discovered it there, but the monks of Newbattle Abbey began to extract it.

It could hardly have been very heart-warming digging away so hard in the belly of the Lowther Hills only to emerge at night to see what wonderful scenery one had been missing. Nor could it have been much fun staying upwind of the smelting sites. Dorothy Wordsworth was one of a number of people who commented on skin problems among children in Wanlockhead: she visited in 1802.

The tombstones in Leadhills cemetery testify to the early deaths of many workers, too. Some were killed underground (there's still a bell on a wooden scaffolding, which was rung to warn of an accident in the mines). Others died young, having been systematically poisoned by the lead fumes from the smelters. In 1982, moreover, environmental health officials admitted that the levels of lead in villagers' blood were equivalent to those expected of city dwellers. One person in twenty in 'God's Treasure-House' has more than the maximum safe level of lead in his or her blood. Wind blown dust from the spoilheaps has continued to be a problem, and the Scottish Development Agency has undertaken a treatment programme.

Another, more offbeat, set-back to living at Wanlockhead was experienced by the lead-miners in 1803 when they intended to form themselves into an early Home Guard in case the French forces invaded them. Their spokesman Gilbert Laing stated: 'The miners are ready to be trained to what exercise is thought necessary; the only difficulty is to find a tolerably flat piece of ground within six miles of the mines, proper to exercise even a company of Pioneers (which as miners we are well adapted to) to be able to march without confusion, may perhaps be thought all that is requisite.' It would have been a zany spectacle indeed seeing hundreds of brawny diggers marching into one another; but it would probably have been odder still seeing them yomping up the Mennock Pass, each of them armed with a pick, shovel and full pack.

Wanlockhead's prosperity peaked a century ago, when the population was 788, six times the present one. The mines eventually shut in 1934, and an attempt by a consortium led by Rio Tinto Zinc to re-open them met with only short-term success.

Nowadays tourism accounts for nineteen per cent of all the jobs in Wanlockhead and Leadhills (its estranged twin a mile or so away, but over the border in Lanarkshire). Tourism nets the local economy £150 000 a year. The Museum of Scottish Lead

View of Beam Engine in 1890, Wanlockhead *(Courtesy: Wanlockhead Museum Trust)*

Loch Nell Visitor Mine, Wanlockhead Museum *(Courtesy: Wanlockhead Museum Trust)*

Mining attracts 35 000 visitors a year, the driving force being Geoff Downs-Rose, a retired miner who acted as unpaid part-time curator from 1974 to 1989. Because of his enthusiasm Pates Knowes, the only surviving smelt-mill in Scotland, has been conserved. So too has the water-powered Beam Engine, the only example of its kind left in Scotland – and a scheduled industrial monument. It was built to drain the Straitsteps mine.

The mining museum exhibits the relics of 250 years of lead-mining, and includes a miner's kitchen and a display of countless minerals. Loch Nell, a walk-in mine, runs under Wanlock Dod, the hill above Wanlockhead where a mine was worked during the eighteenth and nineteenth centuries.

The museum is run by a trust which began with funds of £10. At the time of writing, their coffers were fairly deep, and extensions were being planned.

You could add to Wanlockhead's credits the fact that it had Britain's first community council. And the Wanlockhead Miners' Library is Britain's second oldest subscription library, the oldest being in Leadhills.

Wanlockhead also once boasted Britain's oldest and longest-serving youth hostel warden: Isa Young, who retired on health grounds in December 1987. There must be countless photographs world-wide of cheery Isa who spent fifty years welcoming visitors to Scotland's highest youth hostel.

When I talked to her she had vivid memories of Glaswegians toiling up the Mennock by bicycle without batting an eyelid. When they got to the top they would unstrap their skis and take to the hilltops. She told me: 'Now folk arrive by motor, and the first thing they ask is where the nearest pub is.'

Isa put her longevity down to a strict observance of the work ethic, but I am convinced there must be something in the air up there. You see, in Leadhills there is an unusual tombstone to John Taylor, a surveyor in the lead mines who lived until he was 137. They say when he turned a hundred, his family took him to the highest hill so that God could notice him and take him to Him. However, the old man lived in the village for at least another thirty years. He had no birth certificate, and evidence points to his having been only 134, rather than 137. But then, why spoil a good tale!

Leadhills kirkyard

The hill where they are supposed to have taken Taylor is now the site of a radar station. It was once called 'No Lairds' Land' because it was the burial site of suicide victims. Bodies were carted from great distances to be interred at the border of Lanarkshire and Dumfriesshire. Owing to the taboo about taking one's own life, a graveyard was thought no place for criminals.

The bodies were treated with disdain according to John Brown in Tait Ramage's *Drumlanrig Castle and the Douglases.* He

Michael Ancram, former MP, at the opening of the 212-mile-long Southern Upland Way, which crosses Dumfries and Galloway and the Borders *(Courtesy: Dumfriesshire Newspaper Group)*

wrote: 'In accordance with the dark superstitions of the time, the unblest corpse was treated with curious indignity – no dressing with grave clothes, no striking of the pitiful limbs; the body was thrust with the clothes it was found in, into a rude box, not even shaped like a coffin, and hurried away on some old shattered cart or sledge, with ropes for harness.

'One can imagine the miserable procession as it slunk, often during night, through the village, and past the farmsteads, everyone turning from it as abhorred. Then, arrived at this high and desolate region, the horse was taken out, and the weary burden dragged with pain up to its resting place.'

Suicidal is the way some observers describe the lack of a sewerage system in Wanlockhead, given present plans for an upgrading of the tourist facilities. There's the lure of the Lowther Hills. There is talk of Wanlockhead and Leadhills being turned into a ski-ing centre. And, in 1988, two separate firms of consultants were predicting great things for the villages. The Sanquhar to Beattock section of the Southern Upland Way is nearby. The area has the two oldest subscription libraries in Britain. The colourful industrial history and the magnificent scenery of the Mennock, Dalveen and Enterkin Passes, will surely be a potentially powerful magnet for visitors.

Unfortunately, there are only two Portaloos. The primitive sanitation of Wanlockhead has been lamented by villagers for half a century – ever since the MP, the late Sir Harry Fildes, said that no civilised country could deny the village the basic amenities.

Three months before the implementation of the Community Charge (poll tax) in Scotland, Wanlockhead Village Council were clamouring for a meeting with Scottish Office Minister Ian Lang (their MP), to ask him what they were going to get for their money. Dumfries folk have the same bills to pay and Wanlockhead 'yins' saw it as an extra stick with which to beat the regional council into action. Since their home village had not yet been plumbed into the twentieth century, they were preparing an action plan for the infrastructure and threatening to bring in the European Parliament. No one could blame them.

In a report commissioned by the Scottish Development Agency (SDA), the regional and district councils, British Coal and the Manpower Services Commission, Firn Crichton and Roberts of Edinburgh recommended environmental improvements both to improve the residents' quality of life and to support the village's tourist potential.

An extension of the highest conventional railway in Britain, the two-feet-gauge track, from Elvanfoot to Wanlockhead was another recommendation. A stretch of it had been reconstructed by volunteers out of a dismantled industrial railway from Norfolk: a dedicated team had helped finance it by selling off track certificates at a tenner a time, each paying for another yard of the line. The original Caledonian branch line had been constructed by Robert McAlpine and Sons (who also built the West Highland Line) to carry lead and passengers to the main line. It reached Leadhills in 1901 and Wanlockhead in 1902. The demise of the lead industry shut the line in December 1938. One of the relics is a fine eight-arch viaduct built on a curve.

Back to 1989: Land Use Consultants (LUC) in Glasgow, who were commissioned by the SDA to produce a development plan for Leadhills and Wanlockhead, recommended a five-year-plan costing £2 million. Their report recognised: 'The costs of improvements in basic services have been so high per head of population that it has been difficult to justify the expenditure when equivalent sums spent in more populous areas would benefit more people. On the other hand, if little or nothing had been done, the communities would have been disadvantaged to a still greater extent and the eventual costs in social and economic terms of resettling the communities elsewhere would have posed even greater difficulties.'

LUC reckoned that the villages were a special case which deserved special attention because of their long history of decline. The company suggested that one of the obstacles to a concerted approach for Leadhills and Wanlockhead was the fact that the former was ruled from Glasgow and the latter from Dumfries. The Wheatley Report in 1972 had recommended that Wanlockhead should be part of Strathclyde, but the Local Government Boundary Commission for Scotland overruled it.

Local landlords may well have twisted a few arms. The county boundary marks the boundary between Hopetoun and Buccleuch Estates, and Buccleuch Estates' annexation to Glasgow would not have been in their favour. Quite the reverse. Another explanation was offered to me by Richard Ellam, who became the mining museum's first ever curator in 1989. He quipped: 'It may have been like the Middle East. Some would rather be neglected by Israel than pampered by Egypt!'

When I spoke to Stockport-born Richard, he was preparing for a special exhibition for October 1989 to mark the Burns

Festival run by Nithsdale District Council. Yes, you've guessed it: Scotland's highest village has a connection with the poet. Burns visited it often to collect duties on the silver extracted from local lead. On one particularly icy day in the winter of 1788, he called in at the smithy to get his horse's shoes sharpened in order to give her a better grip on the steep roads of the Mennock Pass. The blacksmith was too busy sharpening tools, and Burns lodged overnight at Ramage's Inn, where he put together a sarcastic little epistle to John Taylor, the mine manager. It went:

With Pegasus upon a day
Apollo, weary flying,
Thro' frosty hills the journey lay,
On foot the way was plying.

Poor, slipshod, giddy Pegasus
Was but a sorry walker,
To Vulcan then Apollo goes
To get a frosty caulker.

Obliging Vulcan fell to work,
Threw by his coat and bonnet
And did Sol's business in a crack –
Sol paid him with a sonnet.

Ye Vulcan's sons of Wanlockhead,
Pity my sad disaster!
My Pegasus is poorly shod,
I'll pay you like my master.

The poem had the desired effect. John Taylor was a big shot in the village, and he persuaded the blacksmith to get Peg Nicholson properly shod for the subalpine conditions. The Smithy is now the site of the lead-mining museum.

Burns next ventured to Wanlockhead in 1792 with Walter and Maria Riddell – on an exploration of the mineshafts. It was to have a damaging effect on his already-deteriorating health. The bard left no written account of the visit. For that we have to rely on Maria Riddell's letter to her mother about 'an expedition not very dissimilar, I think, to that of the memorable Don Quixote in the Cave of Montesinos'.

The trio rose before the sun in the dreary month of January, and breakfasted in Sanquhar. They arrived in Wanlockhead in a post-chaise. Wrote Mrs Riddell: '. . . and the beauties of the majestic scenery joined to the interesting remarks and fascinating conversation of our friend Burns, not only beguiled the tediousness of the road, but likewise made us forget its danger; for it borders the edge of a profound precipice, at the bottom of which a clear brook guides its rapid course over a pebbly bed intersected with rocks.'

A miner led the party into a cavern with tapers in their hands. The roof was so low they had to stoop and wade through clay and water. Stalactites dripped on their heads past the slimy beams.

'After we had proceeded about a mile in the cavern, the damp and confined air affected our fellow adventurer Burns so much that we resolved to turn back, after I had satisfied my curiosity by going down one of the shafts,' added Mrs Riddell. 'This you will say was a crazy scheme – assailing the Gnomes in their subterranean abodes! Indeed there has never before been but one instance of a female hazarding herself thither.'

God's Treasure-House has other literary connections. Many writers visited the oldest library in Britain – founded in 1741 by the poet Allan Ramsay, a native of Leadhills. Ramsay's works include *A Tea-Table Miscellany* and *The Gentle Shepherd,* which subsidised the establishment of the library. The site of his house is open to question, one theory being that it was one of the outbuildings of the Hopetoun Arms Hotel. His name is kept alive in the Ramsay Institute, and a street in the village is named after him.

And the library – many of the original books read by Britain's best-read workmen, are now in the hands of the National Library of Scotland or in Edinburgh University Library, but there are still stacks of useful memorabilia for the thinking traveller. It is still possible to join the library.

Last century Leadhills library opened its doors to people from the cities. Dr John Brown, the author of *Horae Subsecivae,* was a member. So was James Braid, a surgeon and mesmerist who is credited with the introduction of the word 'hypnosis' to the English language.

The Revd Sampson, who was the prototype of Scott's Dominie Sampson, was a subscriber, and the Wordsworths and Coleridge called in 1803. Miss Wordsworth, in fact, wrote an account of her sojourn in her *Recollections of a Tour made in Scotland,* a copy of which is available in Leadhills library.

The entourage of poets found the road blocked by a tree stump, but a crowd of local men shoved it off the road for them. According to Miss Wordsworth: 'They were decently dressed and their manners decent: there was no hooting or impudent laughter.'

So you will have seen that Wanlockhead and Leadhills possess as rich a history as any settlement in the south of Scotland. And they have a tremendous potential for development. According to Geoff Downs-Rose, they stand comparison with any similar place in the British Isles. However, they have been lamentably neglected, and their future rests on political will. When I spoke to Isa Young about how she survived the bleak winters in Scotland's highest village, she gave me an answer which the village council will find appropriate in their predicament: 'Ye git used to everything after a while, bar hingin.'

CHAPTER 13

Sons of Toil

Two thousand ordinary folk took to the streets of Dumfries in 1957 to protest at rent levies imposed on their families by the gentry on the county council. The fight against the rents was to last two years and many of the leading lieutenants in the battle were miners from Upper Nithsdale. The pits are now long gone, but the independent spirit remains, as does local pride that the rent dispute, which almost led to a national strike, filled the headlines of national newspapers and earned a mention in the sober *Third Statistical Account of Dumfriesshire.*

The tenants won a moral victory against the 'toffs', weeks before a test case brought by a Kirkconnel miner, Eugene Weir, was due to be heard in the Court of Session.

What had all the fuss been about? By proclamation of the moneyed folk, a levy of fifteen shillings a week was to be paid by every person in a council house over twenty-one (apart from the tenants and their wives). Ten shillings was to be raised from eighteen to twenty-one year olds. The levy was on the landward areas of Dumfriesshire. It was like a red rag to a bull. There was no justification.

After a rally in April 1957 the council reduced the levies to ten and five shillings respectively. But the tenants refused the means test. Miners, factory workers, farmworkers and housewives boarded special buses to Dumfries from all ends of the county to attend demonstrations.

When the Sheriff in Dumfries arrested the wages of three miners, all hell broke loose. There was a strike involving 1500 miners – and the threat of a national strike. It was labelled 'the most vicious attack on the standard of the working class that has ever come from any local authority'. The rents scheme was the most severe in Scotland, and one tenant wrote to the local newspaper to condemn it as an example of 'mail-fisted Tory robbery'. Tenants fought the May 1957 council elections and Hugh Gaitskell the Labour leader sent his blessings, saying their manifesto had the spirit of the Labour Party's. Few were elected: rural Dumfriesshire was then still cap-in-hand to the aristocrats.

John Lamont, who was president of the Tenants' Defence Association, and now lives at Morecambe, was an electricity meter reader during the dispute. And he well remembers the gentry refusing him entry to their houses to read their meters, so incensed were they at the revolt. He has other stories to relate. For instance, the week his wages were seized, his wife won a box of groceries in a rally raffle. He remembers, too, enjoying a pheasant he had knocked down with his Hillman van, and which had belonged to one of the landowning councillors.

'Councillors tried to intimidate tenants into signing their rent missives any way they could. When a deputation went to the council convener, they all got drunk on his whisky and came back to ask everybody to sign the missives,' recalls John. 'Next time I went along, and shifted the bottle of whisky off the table. It stayed on the sideboard until after the business had been conducted. Three bottles were drunk at the conclusion of the business and I, a teetotaller, was left to drive home.'

Thirty years after the rent strike, Upper Nithsdale is Scotland's worst unemployment blackspot. In January 1987, one in three males of working age was registered on the dole although the area qualifies as a Development Area. Pit closures have taken their toll both on the economy and the look of Kirkconnel. The doors of the last colliery slammed shut in the early 1970s. And the depression is only alleviated by the presence of Brock's Fireworks and Century Aluminium.

The authorities set up the Upper Nithsdale Area Initiative in 1988 to tackle the problems of multiple deprivation, following a report by a team of consultants. Labour councillors claimed publicly that it was in danger of becoming a cosmetic exercise since the Press were banned from meetings. Bert Saunders, the district councillor for Kirkconnel, went so far as to call it 'a conspiracy against democracy'.

The consultants, however, want to see new business workshops, the planting of community woodlands and general environmental improvements. The slag-heaps need screening. Initial capital of £250 000 and £35 000 a year are being earmarked for the Youth Training Scheme (YTS) workshop in Kelloholm, Kirkconnel's satellite.

Sanquhar Post Office *(Courtesy: Dumfriesshire Newspaper Group)*

Kirkconnel and Sanquhar are scheduled to be by-passed in 1993, making consideration of their future imperative. On the tourism front, with the help of the Museums Council, the Scottish Tourist Board and others, there are hopes that Sanquhar Post Office will be developed into a popular port-of-call on the Scottish travellers' trail. It is Britain's oldest post office, dating back to 1763 when 'Post Boys' were hired to deliver mail on horseback. Some claim it is the oldest post office in the world to be used continuously. A replica of its frontage was crafted by Kelloholm workshop for the Glasgow Garden Festival in 1988.

Another potential tourist attraction is the Sanquhar Visitor

Centre or Tollbooth, beloved by local historians but loathed by lorry drivers on the A76 because it juts out into the middle of the road and slows traffic to a standstill.

Nithsdale District Council received a grant of £143 000 from the European Commission towards developing the Tollbooth, which was built in 1735 to replace its crumbling predecessor. It is considered to be one of the best examples of an early Georgian tollbooth in the country. Attributed to William Adam and financed by the third Duke of Queensberry, it stands on the west end of the High Street.

Kirkconnel is relatively short of history of the textbook kind, although its transformation from a rustic village to Dumfriesshire's premier industrial town wove a fascinating social tapestry of its own. *The Statistical Account of Scotland* (1794) lists sixteen collieries, but the first deep-mining operation began in the late 1840s with the sinking of the Gateside pit to twenty-six fathoms. The Bankhead coalfield was opened a decade later, and another was developed at Gateside in 1891. The first pit at Fauldhead was started in 1896, which marked the beginning of the coal-mining heyday. There were seven seams of coal in the Upper Nithsdale coalfield over a finger-shaped basin nearly eight miles long. In 1955 it produced 454 000 tons.

At the end of the First World War, there were 2000 miners winning coal at Fauldhead alone: the population of Kirkconnel had soared from 500 to 4000 within twenty years. Many families had sons, daughters, brothers-in-law and lodgers all under the same roof, and the community atmosphere led to by-names such as 'The Bum' and 'The Glutton'. Later this century, while wee boys followed the Sanquhar-bound coal-carts for pickings for their mammies, the menfolk played quoits and reared pigeons in their spare time. The Kirkconnel Co-op, known in town as 'The Store', was the focal point of activity on Pay Night – when old debts had to be settled and new ones incurred.

There are many fables and vignettes about Kirkconnel life. Consider the 1930s tale about the man who went to see the county council factor about his new house. The factor sighed: 'Not another complaint about draughts?' The reply: 'No, I've come to see if you'll saw a few inches off the bottom of my kitchen door.' Factor: 'Saw off, what do you mean?' Tenant: 'Well, the cat's aye chasing a mouse below it, and it scrapes the fur off her back.'

There's also the tale of the miner who regularly took a raw ham-bone down the pit, and he'd gnaw away at it while his colleagues wolfed their pieces. Then there was the engine-man at Bankhead colliery called Willie Cowan. He used to feed his crusts to the gulls. He stepped out of the door one day to give them their lunch and was killed when a chimney stack fell on top of him.

What about the woman who saw there was a good film on at the local cinema? She sent her children out to get half a dozen bottles of lemonade on tick. She poured the contents into a bucket and sent the weans back to get the deposit on the bottles. You hear all these stories if you mix with the old miners at Mac's Bar or in the bowling club.

They'll tell you about 'Wee Davie Robertson' who did as much as anybody this century for Kirkconnel. He was union man from 1905 till 1951 and was awarded the MBE in 1948 – the year after he unfurled the flag of the National Coal Board when the pits were nationalised. Wee Davie was a school governor, a member of the education committee for thirty-five years, a county councillor and chairman of the parish and district councils. He died in 1953.

Another great worthy was Dr Bowman Edgar, president of the local football team, Kello Rovers, of the horticultural society and of the pipe band. A tale survives of the time he visited a farmer to see his ailing cow. The farmer was giving the cow whisky to get it better. Quoth the medic: 'Don't give her any more. Give me the bottle instead. I'll send you over one of mine in its place. It's not as good a brand, but the cow won't notice the difference.'

There was a tragic side to life in a mining community, of course. Before Parliament acted in 1799, all colliery workers were bondservants, and their lives were negotiable by the mine owners. The capitalists had to give their permission for them to leave their workplace. Tramps, thieves and whole families of poor people became slaves to the owners, and children were sold into bondage to make money. Those who went absent without leave were flung into jail or chained to the wall in a

Jimmy Douglas, Kelloholm, the oldest surviving local miner, unveiling the memorial in Kirkconnel to Upper Nithsdale miners *(Photograph: Andrew McDowell, Sanquhar)*

spring collar. Sometimes they were fastened to a gin with their faces to the horse; their hands were tied behind their backs, and they were forced to run backwards all day. They were chattels to be sold or inherited.

There were accidents underground as well. A geological fault and other circumstances led to many deaths. And in 1984 – fittingly during the miners' strike – a memorial was unveiled in Kirkconnel in memory of those who died. The memorial has a miner's Davey Lamp and helmeted head on top and is a unique tribute to the 'sons of toil' as the local poet, 'Cushie Knowe', called them.

Cushie Knowe, real name Robert Mathieson, was the man behind the application to Nithsdale District Council to erect a monument to the miners. A former deputy at Fauldhead, he

Bob Williamson unveiling the plaque to Alexander Anderson at Kirkconnel station *(Photograph: Andrew McDowell, Sanquhar)*

was anxious to remind future generations that mining was an integral part of their native heritage.

Another, more famous, Kirkconnel poet – whose monument stands in the town cemetery – wrote under the *nom-de-plume,* The Surfaceman. Alexander Anderson was born in the village in 1845, the youngest of six children of a quarryman. He worked as a surfaceman on the old Glasgow and South Western railway for eighteen years. Anderson became librarian at Edinburgh University, having taught himself a number of languages; and he stayed in the job for twenty-nine years. One of the best-known nursery rhymes in the Scottish dialect, *The Bairnies Cuddle Doon at Nicht* was his creation. His *Songs of Labour* sold 2000 copies within a fortnight. The Surfaceman died in 1909: he is remembered by a rugged block of sandstone on Kirk Brae and the inscription, 'He sleeps among the hills he knew'.

Another poet, James Hyslop, who wrote *The Cameronian's Dream,* is commemorated by a red granite obelisk near Whitehill Farm on the banks of the Crawick Water.

Sanquhar's ties with Dumfriesshire are closer than those of Kirkconnel which tends to gravitate towards Ayrshire. Robert Burns called Sanquhar 'Black Joan frae Crichton Peel, O gypsy kith and kin', and he was made a Freeman and burgess of the town in December 1794. During his commuting days to see Jean Armour he would lodge at the New Inn, which became the Queensberry Arms and is now a shop.

In January 1789, though, the poet was ejected from the inn to make way for the funeral cortege of Mary Oswald of Auchencruive, whose late husband had earned a fortune as a plantation owner in Jamaica. The spitefully satirical ode which Burns put together in his head during his twelve-mile-long ride in the freezing weather to another inn at New Cumnock, was described by Thomas Carlyle as something which 'might have been chanted by the Furies of Aeschylus'. Burns's correspondent, Mrs Dunlop, asked him: 'Are you not a sad, wicked creature to send a poor old wife straight to the devil because she gave you a ride on a cold night?'

Sanquhar is also noted as the birthplace of the medieval scholar and adventurer, James Crichton, whose versatility and genius acquired him the nickname, The Admirable Crichton. Crichton was born in 1572 at Elliock House south of Sanquhar and entered St Andrew's University when he was twelve. By the time he was seventeen he was able to conduct public scientific debates in Paris in twelve languages. Crichton was also an

The Marquis of Bute unveils the Crichton tablet in St Bride's Church, Sanquhar *(Courtesy: Dumfriesshire Newspaper Group)*

accomplished swordsman, a poet, a scholar and a dancer. He served in the French army and made a name for himself at the Italian universities. However, 'the Admirable Crichton' came to an abrupt end when he was twenty-two, reputedly at the receiving end of a sword belonging to the Duke of Mantua's son. Crichton had been his tutor, but they had fallen out in a street brawl.

Sanquhar Castle, also on the southern edge of town, stands in ruins today, but in its time it was the formidable seat of the Duke of Queensberry and the site of a well-known siege during the wars of independence. According to the chronicles of Blind Harry, one of William Wallace's men, Sir William Douglas, captured it from English hands. One of Douglas's followers impersonated a woodcutter called Anderson who regularly delivered fuel to the fortress.

The impostor stabbed the turnkey and according to McDowall: 'As they passed to the inner court a desperate attempt was made by the startled garrison to stop the impetuous intruders. "Down with the drawbridge! Lower the portcullis!" cried many a voice; but even if the dying porter's ear had not been adder-deaf, and his hand had not been powerless, the requests could not have been obeyed. The wagon had been intentionally driven forward in such a way that the iron door could not be lowered; and the assailants had already crossed the drawbridge. They appeared in such numbers, and the garrison was taken at such a disadvantage that only a feeble resistance was offered. All the defenders together with their captain were put to death – a doom which they had provoked by their cruel treatment of the inhabitants of the district.'

In the fourteenth century the castle fell into the hands of the Crichtons, ancestors of the Earls of Dumfries, and they renovated and extended it. James VI was entertained there in 1617, and it was sold in 1639 to William Douglas, Viscount Drumlanrig. The second Duke of Queensberry abandoned it and its stones were used to build the aforementioned Tollbooth. Queensberry's descendant, the then Duke of Buccleuch, sold the castle to the Marquis of Bute in 1896.

Sanquhar's hosiery industry brought prosperity to the town until it was affected by the American War of Independence: its chief outlet had been Virginia. Glove-making started off as a cottage industry in Sanquhar in the eighteenth century and today the town's distinctive patterns are sold over the world. There's the Duke pattern, the Rose and the Midge and Fly – all made in accordance with a secret pattern nodded down through the ages. The gloves are usually black and white with the owners' initials woven into the cuffs.

It has been said that the late Helen Shannon of Sanquhar made a special pair for Sir Winston Churchill during the war. Lady Churchill sent her a letter saying he had lost one of the gloves, so she proceeded to knit him another pair.

Mrs Shannon, nicknamed Granny, also knitted gloves for MPs. She told a women's magazine in the 1960s: 'Och weel, it wouldnae do at all for the poor bodies to get cauld feet when they're standing up for Scottish rights way down there.' Why she thought MPs wore gloves on their feet, nobody will ever know.

Footnote:
Mary, Queen of Scots is said to have worn a pair of Sanquhar gloves on her terminal flight from Scotland.

CHAPTER 14

The Nithsdale Covenanting Trail

The normally tranquil village of Moniaive in western Nithsdale was bustlingly chock-a-block on 29 May 1988 for a special, and peculiarly moving, ceremony – a 300th anniversary tribute to the last of the Covenanting martyrs, James Renwick.

Renwick was like the proverbial shepherd who perished in a blizzard within sight of his farmstead: he was executed in the Grassmarket in Edinburgh within months of the so-called Glorious Revolution which ousted the Stuarts and brought an end to the Killing Times. Had William of Orange arrived on the scene ten months earlier Renwick would have been hailed as a national hero rather than being suspended on the gallows.

Nithsdale had been one of the heartlands of resistance to the imposition of bishops – as many rude cairns and memorials on hillsides and moorlands throughout the district will testify. Many southern Scots signed the National Covenant of 1658 against Charles I's claim to be head of the church – with bishops holding sway beneath him.

The whole fabric of religion sown by the likes of John Knox was unravelled and when Charles II reneged on his signing of the Solemn League and Covenant, a twenty-year reign of terror began which saw thousands of defenders of freedom of religion in Dumfries and Galloway put to death by ruthless mercenaries. Bloody Claverhouse (or Bonnie Dundee to his supporters) and Butcher Turner had a field day. Daniel Defoe estimated that some 18 000 Covenanters died. Some, who escaped with their lives, sustained permanent mental and physical torment from long years in colonial dungeons. Protestant uprising after uprising was mercilessly quelled.

Nithsdale villages saw their share of troubles. Today if you drive due west out of Moniaive a splendid monument twenty-five feet high can be seen half a mile from the B729 junction. It is in memory of Renwick who died for the cause, a callow twenty-six-year-old. One writer put it: 'In Richard Cameron they had the Mighty Agitator; in James Renwick they were to receive the Masterly Organiser.'

They say Renwick was praying by the time he was two, so it is unastonishing that he did not graduate from Edinburgh University because he refused to sign the oath of subjection to royal supremacy.

Renwick made for Groningen in Holland to finish his training for the ministry. And as James Dodds, the author of *The Scottish Covenanters,* wrote: 'What was said of Luther, that in his monk's cell he went through within his own soul the whole struggles of the Reformation, may be adapted to Renwick.

'In his student's chamber at Groningen, he went through within his own soul the struggles of the Covenanting cause in Scotland.'

When he returned to Scotland, Renwick published the defiant *Apologetical Declaration,* in which the Covenanters resolved to defend themselves to the death against 'the cruel tyrant, Charles Stuart'.

The Government retaliated by obliging everybody to renounce the declaration, or face their maker. Renwick became public enemy number one, and a price was put on his head. Cottages and cellars throughout the south were turned upside down: ceilings were even pulled down as the dragoons sought the fugitive. He travelled incognito, chased like a partridge in the hills. The mist and midnight were his friends.

Renwick was caught in Edinburgh at a safe house owned by a Cameronian merchant called John Lookup. He went to his death calmly and with dignity – having admitted denying the King's authority, preaching the unlawfulness of paying Cess (the war-tax), and counselling his followers to come armed to conventicles or field-meetings.

His mitigation: 'I own all authority which has its prescriptions and limitations from the word of God; but cannot own this usurper as lawful king, seeing both by the word of God such a one is incapable of rule, and also by the ancient laws of the Kingdom, which admit none to the Crown of Scotland until he swear to defend the Protestant religion, which a man of his profession cannot do – as to the Cess exacted to the present usurper, I hold it unlawful to pay it, both in regard it is oppressive to the subjects for the maintenance of tyranny, and because it is imposed for the suppression of the gospel.'

The martyr's last words were penned on 17 February 1688 to

Monument erected in 1988 to commemorate the tercentenary of the death of the Revd James Renwick executed in Edinburgh 17 February 1688 *(Photograph: George Scott, Cumnock)*

Sir Robert Hamilton: 'I go to your God and my God. Death to me is as a bed to the weary.'

So ended the life of James Renwick, the son of a Moniaive weaver.

The official Nithsdale Covenanting Trail passes Renwick's monument on its way from Caerlaverock to the hills above

Wanlockhead. In Caerlaverock kirkyard lie the remains of Robert Paterson, the stonemason who devoted the last forty years of his life to repairing the tombstones of the Covenanters. Sir Walter Scott immortalised him as *Old Mortality,* the hero of his eponymous novel. He was found dying in the snow at the village of Bankend and snowstorms prevented his relatives from attending his funeral in 1801. Sixty-eight years later Scott's publishers erected a tombstone over Paterson's grave. His epitaph reads:

> Why seeks he with unwearied toil
> Through death's dim walks to urge his way
> And leave his long-asserted spoil
> To lead oblivion into day.

Sandstone statues of Paterson and his beloved horse can be seen in the grounds of Dumfries museum. In 1989, Nithsdale District Council is considering shifting them into the proposed shopping development in Dumfries since mindless vandals with no pride in their history have whacked off Paterson's horse's ears. An alternative is to leave it in the precincts of the museum and to instal video security cameras. It is particularly ironic that thugs should defile the memorial of a man who gave most of his life to repairing those of other people.

Six miles east of Dumfries off the A75 past Collin is the Rockhall Hotel, which was the headquarters of one of the 'baddies'. Grierson of Lag, the notorious scourge of the Presbyterians, whose remorselessness inspired Sir Walter Scott to make him the prototype of Sir Robert Redgauntlet, lived there. It was the location of *Wandering Willie's Tale.*

In the vaulted chamber of the Rockhall there is a hook on which Lag is said to have hanged many a Covenanter. He also used thumb-screws to extract confessions. To cap it all he rolled victims down a hill in barrels filled with iron spikes and knife-blades.

Lag died of apoplexy at the age of ninety in January 1734, and celebrations were held to mark his demise. Observers are said to have got plastered as they watched his funeral at Dunscore kirkyard in Mid Nithsdale. Legend has it that a corbie (a raven or rook) perched itself on his hearse and followed the cortege to the cemetery (the cortege is said to have

Covenanter's Communion by George Harvey *(National Gallery of Scotland)*

been pulled by a team of Spanish horses which died a few days later). Lag's body was so extraordinarily fat that a window had to be taken out of his house in Dumfries for his body to be lowered on to the street. His house, Turnpike House, with its distinctive spiral staircase, stood next to the former County Hotel on the High Street, but it was pulled down in 1826.

Grierson's great-granddaughter tried to get a huge memorial erected over her ancestor's grave, but the hue and cry was so great that the plans were abandoned.

Lag's other home, Lag Tower – now a ruined keep – stands off the B729 road half a mile north-west of the village of Dunscore.

As part of their celebrations of Dumfries's 800th anniversary in 1986, Nithsdale District Council unveiled a memorial cairn outside the market on the town's Whitesands in memory of John Kirko, who had been shot by dragoons on the 'Sands' in May 1685. A laird in Dunscore parish, he had been implicated in the Pentland Uprising. His grave is in St Michael's churchyard near that of Burns. Other Covenanters in the graveyard include William Welsh and John Grierson; and there is an obelisk there to honour the Dumfries martyrs.

Troqueer kirk on the opposite bank of the River Nith was the domain of the Revd John Blackadder, a 'conventicle' preacher who was imprisoned on Bass Rock; incidentally Grierson of Lag had been born in Dalskairth in Troqueer parish.

Moniaive has a scattering of memorials around its hillsides, including the Martyr's Stone at Ingleston Mains Farm, which stands in tribute to five men who were shot by dragoons. In other villages in Nithsdale there are monuments to fearless 'blanket preachers' who, beneath plaids, addressed their congregations on the moors. Penpont, Closeburn and Tynron (where my grandparents were married) – they all have their cairns and stones to freedom fighters.

One of the least accessible of the memorials is Allan's Cairn, which is perched at 1600 feet above sea level on the boundary of Dumfriesshire, Ayrshire and Kirkcudbrightshire, all Covenanting hotbeds.

Old Dalgarnock churchyard south-west of Thornhill has an inspiring granite cross, which was erected in 1928 in honour of fifty-seven Nithsdale martyrs. And in front of it stands a small stone from Australian sympathisers.

Crichope Linn, an adjacent stop along the trail, is a beautiful and spellbinding wooded gorge a couple of miles from Closeburn. A favourite hideout for Covenanting refugees, it featured in Scott's *Old Mortality*. Scott described it to the poet Allan Cunningham as 'both fearful and beautiful', and in the same conversation at the coronation of George IV in London in 1821, he said: 'The stream jumps down from the moorlands, saws its way into the freestone rock of a hundred feet deep, and in escaping to the plain performs a thousand vagaries.'

Magical Crichope was a popular holiday spot during the Victorian era, although it fell from grace after the closure of the village railway station. It used to be fashionable to carve one's initials on the freestone, which the torrents eat away into whimsical-looking shapes. Cunningham, a poet of no average ability, had been born a few miles from the glen; and it is said that when he was a boy he walked all the way to Edinburgh to get a glimpse of Scott. Therefore it must have been with a certain satisfaction that he told his idol at the coronation that, not only had he visited Crichope Linn many times, but also he had used his skills as a stonemason to carve his name on the rock there.

Modern-day visitors may spend hours probing away at Crichope's well-intentioned graffiti. They won't find Thomas Carlyle's initials, but he certainly visited the spot, and it moved him, uncharacteristically, to verse. Whether it was the sight of the gnarled trees bursting out of the crevices above his head or the sound of the Grey Mare's Tail swishing rhythmically as it cascaded its way a hundred feet beneath him, the Muse of the vale's 'deep, dark, drumlie caverns' enchanted him.

The vale also captivated the imaginations of the Covenanters as they escaped Lag *et al:* it was supposed to be haunted by fairies and the 'little people' are reputed to have held meetings there at Elves' Crag. But the Covenanters were more willing to take their chances with ghosts and goblins than with the wrath of their mortal hunters.

Balfour of Burleigh, one of the hunted, gave his name to Burleigh's Leap after vaulting over a chasm to escape the King's men. There is also Cobbler's Cave, Hell's Cauldron and the Sutor's Seat, the latter so-called because it was the lonely retreat of a local shoemaker who supported the Covenant.

Many people have been mesmerised by Crichope Linn, among them the late James Shaw, who was dominie at Tynron at the turn of the century. He wrote in his memoirs of 'dream-grottoes and sunless abysses for all manner of eyeless monsters'. Shaw also recalled the days when droves of people could be seen walking from Closeburn station to Crichope. He wrote: 'When we invite people to Crichope Glen, we cannot, of course, forecast a single day in the calendar; neither have we any remedy for a fit of dyspepsia if the walk from Closeburn railway station is not suitable medicine.'

Further north is Durisdeer, a hamlet tucked below the stunning Dalveen Pass, and the last resting-place of Daniel McMichael, a Covenanter who was shot dead in cold blood at Lower Dalveen farm after refusing to renounce his support for the Covenant. An obelisk in the farm grounds marks the spot where he was murdered. His epitaph in the village kirkyard reads: 'As Daniel cast was into the lyon's den for praying to God and to men, thus lyon's cruelty devoured me for bearing witness to truth's testimony. I rest in peace till Jesus rend the cloud and judge 'twixt me and those who seeked my blood.

'Here lyes Daniel McMichael, shot dead by Sir John Dalziel for his adhering to the word of God, Christ's kindly government of His House and the Covenanted work of the Reformation against tyranny, perjury and prelacy, 1685.'

Within Durisdeer church are the Durisdeer Marbles, one of the finest pieces of sculpture in Scotland. Sculpted by Flemish artists they represent the recumbent figures of the second Duke and Duchess of Queensberry. Thanks to souvenir-hunters who removed the Garter star and ring – together with one of the duchess's fingers – the figures are visible now only through a wrought-iron screen. Coach parties arrive during the summer to marvel at the marbles, and the kirk's visitors' book has the signatures of Queen Elizabeth the Queen Mother, Princess Margaret, Lord Snowdon, the Duchess of Gloucester, the Earl and Countess of Dalkeith and Neil Armstrong, the first man to set foot on the moon.

In the vault beneath the marbles lie twenty-nine lead coffins containing the remains of the ancient Douglases.

The church was built by the Duke of Queensberry in 1699 on the site of an earlier church first mentioned in the books of the monks of Melrose in the thirteenth century. Before the Reformation, the original church had been a place of worship for pilgrims heading for Whithorn and St Ninian's priory. James IV was one such pilgrim.

The present church has unusual box-like pews which allowed the parishoners to sit like families around a table. Another unusual feature of the building is the annexe on the west side. It is the old parish school, whose windows are now blocked by sandstone. Tradition relates that the last parish schoolmaster to teach in the building refused to leave the premises, and he was forced out when slab-layers deprived him of daylight.

In 1556, Baron John Douglas, son of Archibald of Coshogle, appeared in the church after the murder of Hugh Douglas of Dalveen. He was there to hand over his sword to the relatives of the dead man, and thereby avoid a vendetta.

Still on the Covenanting Trail: Mitchellslacks, a secluded

The Sanquhar Declaration *(Courtesy: Librarian, Glasgow University Library)* farm in the foothills of Queensberry (Nithsdale's highest hill) at the edge of the Ae Forest, was a haven for Covenanters. The Harknesses of Mitchellslacks and neighbouring Locherben, were involved in the Enterkin Pass rescue. The Ettrick Shepherd, James Hogg, was later hired at the lonely hirsel for four years (1803-1807) after losing money in a venture in the Hebrides. Allan Cunningham trudged all the way there from Dalswinton estate with his brother James to seek the company of the tattered exile.

Sanquhar has a notable place in Covenanting history, for it was where two of the most famous events of the Killing Times took place. They were the remarkable Sanquhar declaration by Richard Cameron in 1680 and the equally courageous protestation by Renwick in 1685. An impressive granite monument, on the right-hand side as you enter the town from the south, records the declarations.

Both were nailed to the Mercat Cross in front of excited crowds. Cameron, 'the Joshua' of the Covenanters, chose 22 June, the anniversary of the debacle of Bothwell, to publish his resistance against tyranny. And he chose Sanquhar because it was 'the centre of a spacious martyr field, every parish around it except one having been the scene of a Christian martyrdom'.

That day Cameron and twenty followers rode into town from their hideout in the hills and denounced Charles II. Sick of royals tramping on the spiritual rights of the people, they told the crowd: 'Come what may, and hold silent who list, we must and will publish the truth of this cruel king, protest against his misdeeds, and proclaim in the face of heaven that he has forfeited his claim to the throne and to our allegiance.' So saying they issued their manifesto and took to the hills again. A month later, sixty-three Cameronians, Cameron among them, were slain by Bruce of Earlshall near Muirkirk in Ayrshire.

A paper published in 1680 (a copy of which can be seen in the Ewart Library in Dumfries) calls the Sanquhar Declaration 'a treasonable and bloody paper called the Fanaticks' new covenant' and dismisses the Sanquhar twenty-one as 'the notorious ringleader of and preacher at their field coventicles, accompanied with twenty of that wicked crew'.

CHAPTER 15

Devils on Wheels and in Boats

Oh, to have been a fly on the wall – or rather a rook on a stane-dyke somewhere between Thornhill and Sanquhar on the eve of 6 June 1842. A strategically placed rook would have seen the world's first pedal cyclist biking furiously from his Dumfriesshire home to the destination of Glasgow. Kirkpatrick MacMillan, the mad inventor, the so-called 'Devil on Wheels', had fashioned a revolutionary hobby horse which was to land him in jail when he reached the city.

'Daft Pate', one of the inventor's other nicknames, was blacksmith to the Duke of Buccleuch and lived at Courthill smithy in the parish of Keir. He was a versatile chap. He stood in as local dentist and kept a big jar in his smiddy topped with extracted molars. Not only that: there were no vets within striking distance of Courthill, and Pate ministered to the needs of the parish's dogs, cats, along with those of a wide range of farm animals, notably horses, the breaking in of which he succeeded in getting down to a fine art.

When he built his converted dandy horse, his neighbours thought him eccentric, the way most innovators are treated.

Two years before his historic trip to Glasgow, country folk from throughout Dumfriesshire had already seen Pate's contraption. He clocked up an impressive number of practice-miles – and before long the robust Abraham Lincoln-lookalike was covering the fourteen mile ride to Dumfries within an hour – sometimes with his niece Mary Marchbank (the world's first female pedal cyclist) on his shoulders.

The machine itself had wooden wheels, iron-band tyres and a wooden bar frame. It was propelled by cranks on the back wheel which revolved by swinging rods operated by horizontally rocking pedals. It weighed fifty-seven pounds, and to get himself going Pate had to push himself along with his feet (rather like Barney Rubble in the old Flintstones cartoons). Pate got himself a pair of tackety boots to help out.

Before he made off for Glasgow, his father warned him that they would have him on the gallows. Slightly prophetic: the law

Kirkpatrick MacMillan, from an old sketch *(Courtesy: Gordon Irving, Glasgow)*

caught up with him at the Gorbals after he had knocked down a five-year-old girl who had come sallying out of a close. He was well and truly lifted: both he and his bike were thrown into jail. One of his two brothers, who were schoolmasters in the city, put up bail, but the bicycle had to remain in the cells overnight.

In the morning, Pate MacMillan, the world's first pedal cyclist, was in court on the first ever speeding charge. He was charged with 'having ridden along the pavement on a velocipede in the barony of the Gorbals to the obstruction of the passage, and with having by so doing, thrown over a child'.

The magistrate declared: 'This modern craving for speed is

something to be deplored, I must say. A man riding a machine of two wheels and making it progress without having to touch the ground, I just can't believe it. The highways and byways of this country will soon not be safe to travel on.'

Pate was fined five shillings. Later the magistrate, having seen the bike, congratulated him, told him the world would appreciate him for what he had done, and handed him five shillings out of his own pocket.

His legal ordeal over, Pate left for home. They say he met up with Jock Davidson, an old coachman he had often bumped into at staging-posts in Dumfriesshire. Davidson was travelling to Carlisle with the mail, and Pate challenged him to a bet that he would beat him to Sanquhar. He won the wager since Jock had to make a few stops on the way.

The bold Kirkpatrick MacMillan returned to Courthill and a hero's welcome, his neck unstretched although he had a police record. The Duchess of Buccleuch asked him to show off his invention at a garden party – which he duly did.

Unfortunately, Pate was to make no money out of his invention. A Lesmahagow cooper with a photographic memory robbed him of the glory for half a century. That cooper, Gavin Dalziel, had seen the MacMillan prototype and, remembering every detail, he had proceeded to make a few copies, which he sold at great profit. James Johnston, of the Glasgow Tricycling Club, set the record straight in 1892 after an investigation. As for MacMillan's bicycle, rumour has it that it was sold for scrap to an itinerant pedlar.

MacMillan's epitaph, 'He builded better than he knew', is to be seen on the wall of his former cottage at Keir Mill. Every year many a cycling pilgrim comes to pay homage to the man whom his neighbours had thought daft, but who invented one of the world's most widely used and handy forms of transport.

In 1989, preparations were being made for a cycling museum and a Festival of Cycling at Drumlanrig Castle to mark the 150th anniversary of the invention of the machine which revolutionised travel. As a warm-up the Galloway Cycling Group recreated MacMillan's historic ride to Glasgow as part of Dumfries and Galloway's contribution to the Glasgow Garden Festival. Three penny farthings were part of the group which pedalled from the Whitesands in Dumfries past Keir Mill to Glasgow that rain-soaked Saturday in July 1988. John Taylor, one of the Kirkpatrick MacMillan (KM) 150 organising committee, said: 'Courthill is the seat of the invention of the pedal cycle. It should be an international shrine. We intend to make it so.'

Before leaving the subject of cycling. I must mention James Lennox of Dumfries, who while Provost of the town, cycled from John o' Groats to Lands End eight times, establishing many records. Another Dumfries councillor, Chay Richardson, built the area's first river cycle, which he used to pedal up the Nith to the astonishment of the local populace.

John Grierson, another Nithsdale blacksmith, was also an inventor. They say the Durisdeer smith built the world's first tricycle long before MacMillan had built his bicycle. The trouble was it was so heavy he had to get neighbours to give him a push every so often. Grierson also invented a machine which made staples, but when he tried to get it patented he was told it had already been done. The culprit had been a tramp Grierson had invited into the smithy to get some heat into his billy-can. The tramp had, undoubtedly, been attracted by a sprawling advertisement which Grierson had painted across his house. It read: 'Should thirsty folk want lemonade, they may have it strongly made: Or if they wish, they may have bread and cheese. When seated down their limbs to ease. Or should they wish some more repast, they may have supper, dinner or breakfast.' Look to your laurels, McGonagall!

Dumfriesshire is not only noted for producing the world's first pedal cycle: it also revolutionised maritime travel. Two hundred years ago on 14 October 1788, the world's first steamboat propelled its way at the speed of five miles per hour across a loch carved out of a 'noxious swamp' on Dalswinton estate in Nithsdale. The launch of what the journal *Engineering* nearly a century later was to call 'the mother of a race of giants' attracted great media attention. The local newspaper reported that it had been 'successful beyond the most sanguine wishes of any of the parties concerned'.

The parties concerned were three men with Dumfriesshire associations. Patrick Miller, the laird of Dalswinton, put up the money. His children's tutor James Taylor of Leadhills provided the idea. And William Symington, a young engineer from the

Memorial to Symington, the inventor of the steamboat, in Leadhills

Wanlockhead mines who went on to develop the famous *Charlotte Dundas,* the world's first commercially viable steam-tug, affixed the steam engine to it. After the launch, trials were conducted with a larger vessel which made excursions up the Forth and Clyde Canal in December 1789 and down the River Nith from Kingholm Quay to Glencaple in July 1795.

Miller and Taylor lost interest in the project. The laird had plenty of other things to occupy his mind. A deputy governor of the Bank of Scotland, he invented the carronade, an armament which later helped to repel the French Navy. And he was also a leading agriculturalist who introduced the threshing-mill and the drill-plough to Scotland, as well as being the first to come up with the idea of feeding cows on steamed potatoes. Moreover, Miller introduced fiorin grass to Scotland and built a round tower to mark this. Miller also invented a paddle boat armed with carronades, but the British Navy turned its nose up at it, whereupon the inventor presented it to King Gustav of Sweden. In return the king sent him a golden box containing a packet of Swede seeds. So Miller became the first Scotsman to plant turnips.

Meanwhile, back in the world of steam navigation, William Symington soldiered on despite the technical doubts expressed by James Watt, and despite fears among canal-owners that steam-driven paddle-boats would destroy banks.

However, Lord Dundas, who was governor of the Forth and Clyde Canal, commissioned him to build a boat capable of towing heavy barges. It was named after Dundas's daughter, Charlotte, and on its trial run in 1803 – in the face of a fierce headwind – it towed two seventy-ton barges a distance of some twenty miles within six hours. The canal owners objected loudly, saying boat owners would have to pay for damaged banks. The result was that the *Charlotte Dundas* ended its life ignominiously rotting away in a creek at Baisford.

Symington's future looked rosy, however. The Duke of Bridgewater ordered eight steamboats for the Manchester canal. But the Duke died and the project was scrapped. Symington died in London in 1831 in poverty, a broken man. A grey granite monument stands in his memory overlooking the old churchyard in his home village of Leadhills.

While Symington had been down at heel, Henry Bell, a man whom he had hired as a woodworker in the construction of the *Charlotte Dundas,* struck it lucky. *Bell's Comet,* the first regular steamboat in Britain, was built in Port Glasgow in 1812.

The Dalswinton replica is due to be sited as a tourist attraction somewhere in Dumfriesshire – probably in the proposed new shopping mall in Dumfries town centre, or at a revamped Wanlockhead Mining Museum. The brainchild of David Landale, the present owner of Dalswinton estates, it has been constructed under a Manpower Services Commission Programme employing thirty adults and thirteen youngsters for two years.

Originally Nithsdale District Council had planned to site the Dalswinton boat alongside the Robert Burns Centre on the River Nith in Dumfries, but they took cold feet. The reason was that Inverclyde District Council had warned them of what vandals had done to the replica of the *Comet* in Port Glasgow. The council also pointed out that it had been requisitioned by dossers.

The Burns Centre would have been a useful home for it, considering the poet had been a tenant on Dalswinton estate when it all began. The poet had been on the original list of passengers on the maiden voyage, but scholars have argued forcibly that he would have written about the event if he had been on board. Hugh Paisley, an eye-witness interviewed sixty-six years after the launch, claimed Burns had been standing beside him on the shore of the loch.

CHAPTER 16

The Domain of the Duke

There's a far-fetched Nithsdale legend that Adam and Eve settled in Thornhill after their expulsion from Eden. Its veracity is suspect, to say the least, but twentieth century searchers of paradise could do far worse than lodge for a few days in the 'ducal village'.

The smart, small town has a long association with the Dukes of Queensberry and Buccleuch. Even the impressive pollarded lime trees which line the streets were planted by the sixth Duke of Buccleuch in 1861. Another attractive feature of Thornhill – the work of the Duke of Queensberry in 1714 – is the 'cross', an octagonal monument surmounted by a fluted Corinthian column. Pegasus, the winged horse and emblem of the house of Queensberry, stands at the very top of what many acknowledge to be one of the country's finest crosses.

Thornhill was established a free burgh of barony in 1662 with the name New Dalgarno. And the Duke of Queensberry laid the present settlement out at right angles to the cross. When the author, Dorothy Wordsworth, passed through she recorded: 'the houses are so small that they may have been built to stamp a character of insolent pride on his own huge mansion at Drumlanrig, which is in full view on the opposite side of the Nith'.

William, the first Duke of Queensberry, spent a fortune building Drumlanrig out of pink sandstone on the site of a former stronghold of the Douglases, who were supporters of King Robert the Bruce. The building went up between 1679 and 1690. It took eleven years to build, but – by choice – the Duke slept there only one night.

The fourth Duke of Queensberry was a notorious dandy and gambler who squandered his fortune, but lived to the grand old age of eighty-five bearing the nickname Old Q. He died with many illegitimate offspring, but no legal heir, and that is when Henry Scott, third Duke of Buccleuch, took over the Queensberry line. Thomas the Rhymer had predicted the fall of the house of Queensberry in a couplet running:

Drumlanrig Castle, the Dumfriesshire home of The Duke of Buccleuch and Queensberry KT

When the Mar burn rins where man never saw,
The house of Hassock is near a fa'.

The burn was diverted from its channel into a drain, before old Q's death, and the house of Hassock had been the colloquial name for the old Douglas seat.

Nowadays, Drumlanrig is the home of the current Duke of Buccleuch, who is reputed to be the second largest landowner in Europe. Many visitors come to the castle for its internationally famous collection of priceless art treasures, which includes works by Rembrandt, Gainsborough, Holbein and da Vinci.

There is a Madonna by Leonardo da Vinci which is thought to be the only one by him in a private collection. And the Rembrandt, *An Old Woman Reading*, signed and dated 1655, is a marvellous portrayal of a wise old face – although the 'navvy-like' hands are said to have been finished by one of his pupils.

The castle drawing-room has a unique inlaid cabinet presented by Louis XIV to Charles II, who gave it to his son James, Duke of Monmouth and Buccleuch. A Charles II chandelier weighing nine stones hangs above the oak staircase. There is also an intriguing equestrian portrait of William III which bears slash marks. Bonnie Prince Charlie rested at Drumlanrig with his followers on 23 December 1745 after the abortive rebellion; and some of his Highlanders stabbed their dirks through the picture of the king they hated.

Portraits of the Pretenders hang on either side of the south-facing bedroom window, and some of the Young Pretender's personal relics can be seen, including his rings and a camp kettle. Drumlanrig has other attractions: Flemish tapestries and a tapestry believed to have been the work of Mary, Queen of Scots, who visited the castle. There are also carved friezes, silverware from Wanlockhead and fluted stone balustrades.

Outside, beyond the horseshoe-shaped stairs, there are forty acres of gardens, splendidly landscaped woods with nature trails, Victorian summer-houses and a tree planted by the astronaut Neil Armstrong during his visit to receive the Freedom of Langholm. There are other more noteworthy trees: a weeping beech, one of the country's first Gingko trees, Britain's oldest Douglas Fir, which is 132 feet high, and a massive sycamore. The sycamore, cited in *The Guinness Book of Records* as Britain's largest, consumes up to 600 tons of water per year.

Trees, or at least the felling of them at Drumlanrig, angered the poets Burns and Wordsworth, both of whom wrote scathing verses condemning the devastation of the estates by Old Q to provide a dowry for one of his illegitimate children.

Burns is supposed to have written the following couplet about the matter on a window-shutter in the locality:

> The worm that gnawed my bonny trees
> That reptile wears a ducal crown.

However, according to James Mackay, the respected Dumfries expert on Burns, Henry Mackenzie wrote the words as a Burnsian pastiche. In his excellent work, *Burns Lore of Dumfries and Galloway*, he states: 'He confessed in a letter to Dr James Currie in 1802 that he had invented the tale of the inscription on the window shutter. William Wordsworth visited the denuded policies of Drumlanrig in 1803 and lamented their destruction at greater poetic length.'

Burns lampooned the debauched playboy duke in his *Election Ballad,* and he wrote of him:

How shall I sing Drumlanrig's grace –
Discarded remnant of a race
    Once great in martial story
His forebears virtues all contrasted –
The very name of Douglas blasted –
    His that inverted glory!

Hate envy oft the Douglas bore:
But he has superadded more
    And sunk them in contempt!
Follies and crimes have stained the name,
But Queensberry, thine the virgin claim,
    From aught that's good exempt!

The present occupant of Drumlanrig, the ninth Duke of Buccleuch and the eleventh of Queensberry, has maintained the enlightened approach to conservation fostered by the fifth Duke of Buccleuch. The castle is at the heart of a bustling estate employing several hundred people. It contributes a great deal to the local economy as one of south-west Scotland's foremost visitor attractions.

To return to Burns: he was weel-kent in the Thornhill area. Although he was once assaulted by smugglers outside a Penpont inn, he generally got on well with the people in the region. A Professor Gillespie of St Andrews University wrote of having seen him chap at the door of Kate Watson who ran an illicit shebeen in Old Street, Thornhill.

'Kate, are ye mad? Dinna you know that the supervisor and I will be in upon you in the course of forty minutes? Goodbye t'ye at present.' Gillespie quotes him as having said.

Burns loved his whisky – and resented it being diluted. Another tale is told of his visiting Jean Davidson's pub where the water of life was being watered down. He sampled some and put the royal seal on the barrels telling her he would be back in the morning to collect them. Jean cleverly got a cooper to remove three hoops from the barrel and bored a hole in below, through which the whisky was restored to full strength.

The next day, Burns was baffled when Jean asked him to check it again. 'Was there aught wrong with me last nicht,

Jean?' he asked, after realising the potency of the beverage. Came the reply: 'Weel, Mr Burns, it's really no for me to say, but – weel, I jeest thocht ye were ower smert wi yer tester.'

Thornhill was where the bard bought new shoes. Andrew Johnstone was the man who supplied them from a shop which stood where the Buccleuch Arms stands today. Johnstone, who always said he had never seen 'bonnier een in ony heid' than that of Burns, was late with the footwear once, and he reputedly told a villager, Archibald Maxwell, that he was 'feart he (Burns) would mak poetry about it'.

If Burns was admired by his cobbler, then Joseph Thomson, a native of Penpont, achieved the status of a demi-god in both Penpont and Thornhill, where his parents made their home when he was two. Thomson (who incidentally died at the same premature age as Burns) was to be the first European explorer to penetrate the land of the fierce African Masai warriors – and come out of it alive. The youngest of five sons of a stonemason, he trained as a geologist at Edinburgh University, and by the age of twenty-one he was leading his first expedition, a 3000-mile trek to Lakes Nyasa and Tanganyika. Not a single man deserted, and there was not a shot fired in anger. For a white man in Victorian Africa he was a rare pacifist, believing that a gentle word was more powerful than gunpowder. He tramped through large tracts of Zaire, Tanzania, Kenya, Nigeria and Morocco – and made treaties with the potentates of Zambia and Malawi. History relates that he won the hearts of the ferocious Masais by showing them conjuring tricks. One writer observed: 'He would charm them with mirrors and his own false teeth and treated their sick with an effervescent mixture of Eno's Fruit Salts.'

Thomson died young, but with a Gold Medal from the Royal Geographical Society under his belt for identifying a tree. His name is commemorated by the Thomson Falls in Kenya and the antelope, called after him – Thomson's Gazelle.

When he died in 1895 he was bracketed alongside Livingstone and Park, fellow Scots, in the first league of British explorers, but his name is obscure today. One influential scientific journal wrote of him after his death: 'With him dies the only traveller of our time who, as regards pluck, his persistence and his methods, is worthy to rank with

Joseph Thomson, the great Penpont-born African explorer *(Courtesy: Royal Geographical Society, London)*

Livingstone.' And the writer of his obituary in *The Times* declared that he belonged to 'an almost extinct race of great African explorers'. Among the pall bearers at his funeral were his great friends, J M Barrie, and the poet, Alexander Anderson (The Surfaceman).

Sir Clements Markham, president of the Royal Geographical Society, unveiled a plaque in his honour in Thornhill in 1897. And there is a monument to him in front of Morton School in Thornhill, where he received part of his education. At Thomson's centenary in 1958, however, the High Commissioner of Kenya insisted that his birthplace of Penpont should steal the limelight for the official celebrations.

There isn't, to my knowledge, any statue to Dr Thomas Grierson, but perhaps there should be. For his enterprise once attracted many tourists to Thornhill to see one of the most unusual museums around. The museum in New Street had a fascinating collection of fossils, but there was much more – a glass jar with opium for curare arrowheads, a cast of Burns's skull, a piece of wood from his coffin and an excise permit in his writing. Even more bizarre to relate: there were snakes in bottles, and a two-headed calf. There were a herbarium, several sixteenth century Bibles and Annandale sandstone with reptiles' footprints.

Grierson was an eccentric with 'a butterfly mind', who built the museum with stones donated by the then Duke of Buccleuch in the early 1870s. He corresponded with Charles Darwin and Thomas Carlyle, and he was an avid naturalist who was often seen out planting exotic shrubs on burnbanks and in local woods.

He was noted for his thriftiness. A local writer, the late Joseph Laing Waugh, recalled spending Christmas morning helping the doctor and his housekeeper to rearrange the library: his hopes of a share in the festive dinner were dashed when the two of them sat down to a cup of tea each and a Finnan haddock between them.

Grierson's museum closed in 1965 after a public enquiry. It had run out of money, and its incredible contents are now dispersed. First choice went to local institutions, and Dumfries museum was one of the recipients. As David Lockwood, curator of the latter museum, put it: 'It seems a sad end to the collection of quite a remarkable man who was regarded with pride and admiration locally and respected as a scholar nationally.'

There have been several 'local heroes' but Elspeth Buchan, the leader of one of the strangest religious sects in Scottish history, must perhaps take the honour for being the most eccentric.

'Mother' Buchan and her fellow believers came from Banffshire and settled in a thirty-foot-wide barn on the farm of New Cample near Closeburn in the middle of the eighteenth century. She had been hounded out of Irvine, Glasgow and Perthshire, one of the reasons being that the locals of each place were none too pleased at her habit of preaching that she was the third person in the God-head and the person described in *The Revelation of St John* as being 'clothed with the sun and the moon'.

Buchan and her right-hand man, the Revd Hugh Whyte, an erstwhile American professor, converted around sixty people in the Thornhill area. But New Cample (Buchan Ha') was attacked by a hundred men with pitchforks and bludgeons on Christmas Eve 1784 following allegations of infanticide. The Buchanites took refuge in Closeburn Castle, which had been the seat of Sir Roger Kirkpatrick, who had been an accomplice in Robert the Bruce's murder of the Red Comyn in Dumfries.

The undoing of the sect was when Mother Buchan ordered them to fast for forty days and forty nights (she was exempt, you understand). The starved followers laboriously climbed Templand Hill on the forty-first day – in their slippers – ready to go to Heaven. Amazingly, they all shaved their hair in a Mohican (or more precisely Huron Indian) style: they were told it would allow the angels to grab them and ease them in through the pearly gates. Equally farcically, Mother Buchan fell off her pedestal and the rich members who had financed the sect drifted away.

Mother Buchan died in 1791 and her body was kept in cold storage by Andrew Innes, of Crocketford near Castle Douglas. He waited for fifty years for her resurrection from the coffin he had hidden in his house, but to no avail. He died aged eighty-nine, having ordered his body to be placed above Buchan's bones. His theory was that if she decided to go to

Edward Martin, master blacksmith from Closeburn *(Courtesy: Dumfriesshire Newspaper Group)*

Heaven, he would be lifted with her. His bones, Mother Buchan's and those of fourteen Buchanites were eventually laid to rest in the corner of the garden of Innes's house. Latterly it was a chicken farm.

Stranger than fiction? Yes, I agree – and there's the predictable connection with our national poet. According to the antiquarian and friend of Sir Walter Scott, Joseph Train, Innes's sister Jean Gardiner was the 'Darling Jean' of the *Epistle to David Sellar* – instead of Jean Armour. There is no evidence to support this other than the fact that Innes had told Train that Burns had tried in vain to get Jean to leave the sect at New Cample.

Closeburn is a mile from New Cample as the crow flies. And it is the centre of the universe every summer for blacksmiths from all over the world. One Saturday each August they go at it hammer and tongs in the biggest one-day horse-shoeing competition in Britain. The event, hosted by Ed Martin, a third generation farrier from the tiny village, is a shop window for a craft which was once threatened with extinction by mechanised farming practices.

Every August the huge Clydesdales stand unmoved as Scandinavians and Americans vie with each other to achieve the perfect equine pedicure. Sparks fly from half a dozen forges as elsewhere a hiss is followed by a whiff of singed hoof.

Ed Martin's great-grandfather set up his forge at Closeburn in 1854, when farriery was the lynchpin of any rural community. As technology took over from brawn, Ed joined them since he couldn't beat them: he opened a garage selling agricultural machinery.

CHAPTER 17

The Bard, the Sage and the Apostles

Robert Burns's arrival as a tenant on the Nithsdale estate of one of the future fathers of steam navigation in May 1788 was relatively inauspicious. Burns had written to the landlord Patrick Miller: 'I want to be a farmer in a small farm, about a plough-gang, in a pleasant country under the auspices of a good landlord.'

However, Ellisland farm with its 170 acres on the right bank of the River Nith in Dunscore parish, was almost to ruin the poet. It had never been a viable proposition: Burns himself had written to John Ballantyne in January 1787, saying: 'Some life-rented embittered Recollections whisper me that I will be happier anywhere than in my old neighbourhood, but Mr Miller is no Judge of the land; and though I dare say he means to favour me, yet he may give me, in his opinion, an advantageous bargain that may ruin me.'

The rent was £50 a year, and he had to build his own house while he stayed in an adjacent cowshed and commuted to Mauchline to see Bonnie Jean. The land at Ellisland was virtually barren. In fact Miller admitted several years later: 'When I purchased this estate about five and twenty years ago, I had not seen it. It was in the most miserable state of exhaustion and all the tenants in poverty.'

The Ellisland years were to be traumatic ones for the bard. The house took an unexpectedly long time to put up, and his first harvest was a disaster. There were other worries, not least how Burns could find time to train as an exciseman, battle against the land and write poetry. Yet at the but and ben – with a sod-dyke for a desk – he composed some of his masterpieces, among them *Auld Lang Syne, John Anderson my Jo* and *Tam o' Shanter*. In addition a third of his extant letters were written during his three-year spell at the farm.

Legend maintains that Burns composed *Tam o' Shanter* in one day (since Bruce fought Bannockburn the best single day's work done in Scotland, as one observer put it). Burns's letters disprove the theory, but the myth persists even on the plaque

Robert Burns by Alexander Nasmyth *(Scottish National Portrait Gallery)*

attached to the gate leading to the riverside walk at Ellisland.

In forceful Victorian journalese, the historian William McDowall advocated the Tam o' Shanter myth – imagining Jean Armour and the two children crouching behind a whin-bush watching the poet pace up and down the path crooning to himself.

'He becomes increasingly excited; his manner is that of a

pythoness, so strange and wild are his gesticulations and, though now at the remote end of the promenade, she can perceive that he is agonised with an ungovernable access of joy. It is his masterpiece of *Tam o' Shanter* with which he is busy,' wrote McDowall in his *History of Dumfries.*

Burns eventually gave up Ellisland in 1791 to concentrate on his customs duties after realising that it had 'undone my enjoyment of myself'. He told his brother Gilbert: 'It is a ruinous affair on all hands. But let it go to hell!'

John Morine, the laird of neighbouring Laggan farm, eagerly took over Ellisland, but there was a row between him and Burns over the price of some dung, which culminated in an incident which deprived posterity of some important Burnsian relics. Hot-tempered Rabbie – also incensed at Morine's insistence that he left fences ship-shape – sent his brother-in-law Adam Armour in with his big boots on to smash every pane of glass which sported the poet's handwriting. The hired vandal received six shillings for his work, and Burns slated Morine in an epigram.

Morine sold Ellisland in 1805, but it has been reasonably conserved to this day as a tourist attraction with resident curators. Farming stopped there in 1921, when a former president of the Edinburgh Burns Club bought it. The parlour is now a museum to the poet, and a granary was restored in the late 1970s and opened as a museum of farming life. The Royal Scottish Museum installed a life-size model of the poet in period garb sowing oats from a sheet over his left arm.

In 1987, Jim and Jean Irving took over as curators at Ellisland – exactly 199 years after Burns had moved in. Jim had, like Rabbie, worked as a ploughman. He was secretary of the Dumfries and Galloway Vintage Machinery Club and a former president of the Dumfries Burns Howff Club.

To mark the 200th anniversary of Burns's flitting to Ellisland, the Ellisland Trust struck a medallion with the poet's head on one side and a picture of the farm on the tail side. It was cast by Tower Mint of London and all profits went towards the upkeep of Ellisland.

Jane Haining was a local hero of a different kind from Burns. Dunscore-born she became a missionary to the Jewish mission in Hungary and died for her beliefs in the Nazi death

Jane Haining, the Dunscore martyr who died in Auschwitz

camp at Auschwitz. Jane was educated at Dumfries Academy where she became Dux of the Modern School during the First World War, the year after the actor John Laurie had come runner-up.

Jane worked for ten years in a threadmaker's in Paisley, but at a meeting in Glasgow about the Jewish Mission she turned to a friend and said, prophetically: 'I have found my life-work.' After a crash course in Hungarian, she took charge of the Girls' Home of the mission in Budapest. The Nazis jackbooted their way into Hungary during the last March of her life, and she wept as she had to sew Stars of David on the youngsters. Gestapo men raided the place. Jane had ignored the warnings of the Church of Scotland to come home to safety, and she was thrown in jail. She refused to reject her children, and it cost her her life.

According to Elizabeth Walker in her husband's book, *A*

Legacy of Scots, Jane Haining was the only Scot to be slain in the Nazi concentration camps, and was probably gassed along with a batch of Hungarian women on 16 August 1944. However, her death certificate reads: 'Miss Haining, who was arrested on account of justified suspicion of espionage against Germany, died in hospital, July 17, of cachexia brought on by intestinal catarrh.'

Two days before her (official) death, Jane had written obsessively to a friend Margit about apples, fresh fruit and bread: she was obviously starving. You can read between the censored lines. She wrote pathetically: 'Even here on the road to Heaven there is a mountain range to climb.'

Now her supporters in Scotland are remembering her words as they try to have her honoured for eternity in the Avenue of Righteous Gentiles in Jerusalem. For her name to be admitted, much first-hand information is needed – an almost impossible task.

The most moving tribute to the Dumfriesshire martyr was written by one of her former wards: 'I still feel the tears in my eyes and hear in my ears the siren of the Gestapo motor car. I see the smile on her face while she bade me farewell. I never saw Miss Haining again, and when I went to the Scottish Mission to ask the minister about her, I was told she had died. I did not want to believe it, nor to understand, but a long time later I realised that she had died for me, and for others. The body of Miss Haining is dead, but she is not alone, because her smile, voice and face are still in my heart.'

Among the memorials to Jane Haining are two stained glass windows in Queen's Park church, Glasgow, where she worshipped, and a plaque in the little kirk of Dunscore, which stands on the site of the one, where Robert Burns prayed most Sundays during his stay at Ellisland.

Burns spent three years of Sundays listening to the 'tortuous and Whiggish' sermons of the Revd Joseph Kirkpatrick, whom Robert Riddell had described as a 'mule' and Burns himself had described to Allan Cunningham as 'one vast constellation of dullness, and from his weekly zenith rays out his contradictory stupidity to the no small edification and elightenment of the heavy and opaque pericraniums of his gaping admirers.'

Burns, a Jacobite in sentiment, was so angry at Kirkpatrick's sermon on the anniversary of the Glorious Revolution that he wrote a scathing essay published in the *Edinburgh Evening Courant* under the pseudonym, A Briton.

I'm sure Burns would have been impressed by Edward Irving, the notorious evangelist who could have out-preached Kirkpatrick. Irving in fact delivered a sermon in Dunscore kirk (the neo-Gothic one erected in 1823), and there were so many people there to see him that the congregation spilled out into the kirkyard.

Among the congregation was Thomas Carlyle, who lived at Craigenputtock in the north-western corner of the parish of Dunscore. Carlyle likened it to the Greek island of Patmos – even although his biographer Froude called it 'the dreariest spot in all the British dominions'. It was at Craigenputtock that the 'Sage' composed his epic *Sartor Resartus* and his much-praised *Essay on Burns.* When the American poet and essayist, Ralph Waldo Emerson, visited the Carlyles he and Carlyle climbed Craigenputtock Hill and talked about German idealism. Carlyle told Emerson as they gazed down on Dunscore church: 'Christ died on the Tree that built Dunscore kirk yonder that brought you and me together. Time has only a relative existence.'

Carlyle's father and Allan Cunningham were employed in building Auldgirth bridge in Closeburn parish, across which Burns must have ridden many a time during his duties as an exciseman. Cunningham was a poet and stonemason of considerable talent, who was granted the Freedom of Dumfries. 'Honest Allan' had been born on the estate of Blackwood (near Keir the birthplace of Kirkpatrick MacMillan). But the cottage where he was born is now long gone. Cunningham is perhaps best known for his outstanding maritime lyric, *A Wet Sheet and a Flowing Sea,* and was a friend of Carlyle, Hogg and Scott.

Burns visited Closeburn Castle many a time to see its factor, William Stewart. There he inscribed a crystal tumbler with the words, Welcome Willie Stewart, which was later acquired by Scott and put on display at Abbotsford House.

Friars' Carse, six miles north of Dumfries, is now a convalescent home for Post Office employees. In ancient times it had been the site of a British fort and a Druidical circle, and in the Middle Ages it had been owned by one of the Cistercian monks of Melrose. The monks used the neighbourhood loch as the fish pond of the friary and its crannog as a harbour for their valuables during English raids.

Friars' Carse was another of Burns's haunts – the home of Captain Robert Riddell, a musician and collector of folk music, who became a bosom friend of the bard. The mansion was the venue of a famous drinking competition immortalised by Burns in *The Whistle,* to which Riddell wrote the music. Three rivals, Alexander Fergusson of Craigdarroch (Bonnie Annie Laurie's son), Sir Robert Laurie of Maxwelton (her nephew) and Captain Riddell (her son-in-law), competed to see who could get drunk last and win an ebony whistle allegedly brought to Scotland by a servant of the Danish royal family. Fergusson won by gorging himself with five bottles of claret. Burns, merely an observer, rode home in a straight line.

So close were the bard and the Riddells that he composed *The Day Returns* in their honour. In the preface he wrote: 'At their fireside I have enjoyed more pleasant evenings than at all the houses of fashionable people in this country put together; and to their kindness and hospitality I am indebted for many of the happiest hours of my life.'

Alas the friendship was broken in 1793 after Burns's reportedly over-enthusiastic rendition of *The Rape of the Sabines* when he was drunk on port. Burns apparently sought carnal knowledge of Mrs Riddell, and he was ordered from the house in disgrace – never to return.

Friars' Carse was later the home of Dr James Crichton whose money was used by his widow to found the world-famous Crichton Royal mental hospital in Dumfries. The mansion was also where Bonnie Annie Laurie, the heroine of the famous love song and the beautiful 'Lady Bountiful of Nithsdale', died at the age of eighty-one in 1764.

Maxwelton House, a splendid fifteenth century mansion near Moniaive, was where Annie was born. It now houses a museum of agriculture and domestic life with an attractive garden and a nineteenth century chapel charmingly located by a small pond. The house incorporates the distinctive round tower of Glencairn Castle.

Maxwelton House, Moniaive, birthplace of Annie Laurie *(Courtesy: Dumfriesshire Newspaper Group)*

Sixty-five men took three years in the 1960s to restore Maxwelton House, and the results of their efforts are worthy of the old lines:

> Maxwelton Braes are bonnie
> Where early fa's the dew
> And it is here that Annie Laurie
> Gied me her promise true.

Holywood, nearer Dumfries, is another interesting place associated with monks, druids and legends. A quarter of a mile from Holywood church stand the Twelve Apostles, the stone circle with the largest diameter on the Scottish mainland, and one of the two almost perfect stone circles in Dumfriesshire (the other being the Girdlestanes of Eskdalemuir). The Apostles – there are only eleven of them left – are believed to have been erected between 1800 and 1600 BC, and tradition associates them with an annual synod held by Druid priests. Their layout suggests an astronomical setting similar to that of Stonehenge.

Holywood parish, which takes its name from the sacred grove which used to cover it, was the site of one of the oldest and most influential monasteries in the county, Dercongal

Abbey. It was founded by John, Dominus of Kirkconnell in the twelfth century.

The monks of the abbey – which occupied the south-western corner of the existing churchyard – held vast tracts of land, but they lost their power during the Reformation. An interesting court case tells of the Abbot's tenants petitioning for an interdict to stop him calling them out on raids so often, because they did not have enough time to get their farming done.

The abbey's old bells have been incorporated into the church, and they are still rung regularly. One of them bears an inscription which proves that it was consecrated by the abbot, John Wrich, in 1154 in the reign of Malcolm IV.

Lincluden Collegiate Church, which is also situated off the A76 on the outskirts of Dumfries, is another important historic building. In fact it celebrated its 600th anniversary in 1989. Many visitors call in to the red sandstone ruin, which houses the tomb of St Margaret with its effigy of the princess resting on a plinth. Lincluden College has had its quota of royal pilgrims, among them Queen Margaret of England, who sheltered there with her son during the Wars of the Roses. In 1505 James IV stayed there during his pilgrimage to Whithorn.

Lincluden had a Benedictine nunnery – until 1389 when Archibald the Grim, third Earl of Douglas, seized it and unceremoniously ejected the sisters. In their place he put in eight priests and a provost.

CHAPTER 18

The Queen of the South

Dumfries, the capital of south-west Scotland, has entertained many monarchs and granted her Freedom to one of them – oddly King Olaf of Norway, whose exiled 'sodgers' were warmly welcomed by the townsfolk who gave them a base during the Second World War. Queen of the South, the local football team which owes its name to the town's other sobriquet, played keen matches against the Scandinavians, a few of whom sported medals awarded in the finals of the Olympic Games. The 'Queens' have tanked the 'Old Firm' (for non-football fans – the Glasgow teams of Celtic and Rangers) in their time, too, in the days when Billy Houliston, now a hotelier in Dumfries, was capable of putting both the ball and the goalie into the net without being shown the red card. Yes, Queens were once the coupons-busters of the old First Division. As I write they have just been relegated to the new second division, having let more goals in than any other professional football team in Scotland.

More than 'fitba' has changed in Burns's 'Maggie by the banks o' Nith' in living memory, though. The area of the town has expanded five-fold since the 1920s, and the multiple chain store owners have moved in to build those hideous, homogeneous things called 'shopping centres'. Gone is the network of stinking closes like Sheepheid Raw, whose undernourished inhabitants had hard-gotten mutton heids singed at the local foundry. Here to stay is the pedestrianised town centre. Scotland's leading property development company, Scottish Metropolitan, started knocking Assembly Street down in 1988 to beat rival firms to get their plant-filled malls up.

Scottish Secretary, Malcolm Rifkind, was in town during the winter of 1988 to cut the first sod of the by-pass, an operation designed to prevent Dumfries's clogged arteries from haemorrhaging during rush-hours. Meanwhile, parking in Dumfries without getting a ticket remains a problem, and 'white settlers' mainly from the Home Counties continue to use their financial advantages over Scottish Lowlanders to buy up houses from the local property supplements as if there were no tomorrow. There are widespread rumours of 'gazumping'. House prices, consequently, continue to soar long after the now-abortive hunt for oil in the Solway Firth was seen as the cause of the influx. Now Dumfries and Galloway is poised to become an overspill from the Lake District circus. Perish the thought!

Les Jardine, Dumfries and Galloway Regional Council's go-ahead director of economic development, has spearheaded trips to the finance houses of Edinburgh and London to try to woo new industry into the area. Meanwhile, Gates (formerly Uniroyal), ICI and Carnation provide employment hopes for the young of tomorrow.

Dumfries's past is also being seen as one of the keys to its future. History – the town is saturated with it – is an important asset which attracts many tourists, Burnsians and ancestor-hunters. Our national poet, Robert Burns, lived, died and is buried here in a town where Robert the Bruce ignited the spark which led to the fire of Scottish independence, by slaying the Red Comyn in Greyfriars' monastery – now a supermarket cellar in Castle Street.

Four hundred years later a spark of a different kind, but also associated with the love of independence, was ignited at the town's Mercat Cross. Masons working on the building of the Midsteeple would have a bird's eye view of anti-Unionists ceremoniously burning the Articles of Union in protest at the selling of Scotland to the English. The event was emulated in 1986 by the SNP candidate for Dumfries at the general election.

In 1745, Bonnie Prince Charlie held the town's VIPs to ransom as he headed north from Derby. The Jacobite camp was pitched in what is now Shakespeare Street, and troops took over the Blue Bell Hotel which was, until recently, the County Hotel.

The Young Pretender used the hotel for a council of war, and one of its rooms was thenceforth known as the Bonnie Prince Charlie room. Ironically, the room is now part of a shoe-shop – ironically, that is, because the prince demanded 1000 pairs of shin for his Highlanders. When these, the sum of

£2000 and horses, carts and ammunition were not forthcoming within twenty-four hours the rebels pulled the shoes off gentlemen's feet in the streets. They also took two hostages to make sure that the sum of £2000 was rendered unto Charlie. It was. But the third Duke of Queensberry was instrumental in getting compensation from the Government – with interest. To thank him, the town council erected a column in his memory in 1780. Because of traffic problems it was moved from Queensberry Square to the front of the county council chambers in 1935. However, in 1989 it is scheduled to be moved back to its original position opposite the snack bar which now occupies the stately Trades Hall. Tom McCallum, an SNP councillor in Dumfries, called for the column to be returned to 'the quarry where it belongs'. According to Tom, the Duke's forebear had been a traitor: he had been the Parliamentary commissioner who had spearheaded the union.

Dumfries was also a prominent seaport until the coming of the railways, and it was for many years the leading market for hare-skins in Scotland. When the Arrol Johnston company were building motor-cars in the factory now occupied by Gates (they produced Malcolm Campbell's *Bluebird*) Dumfries was being forecast as 'the Scottish Coventry'.

The town, however, has other, less glamorous, claims to fame. It hanged the last man and woman to be executed publicly in Scotland. Robert Smith was condemned to die in 1868 after he raped an eleven-year-old girl in a plantation near Annan, strangled her and then robbed her body of nine shillings and elevenpence. He calmly walked into town to buy tobacco and biscuits before attempting to murder a woman near Cummertrees. He shot and stabbed her, but she escaped because two boys came to her door selling turnips from a donkey and cart. What they thought was a parrot screeching was Jane Crichton fighting for her life.

Six hundred people watched Smith being launched into oblivion at the junction of Buccleuch Street and St David's Street. When the body was cut down, the lay preachers scurried away and a Carlisle plasterer, called Rushfirth, rushed forth and took a cast of Smith's skull. The cast is now in Dumfries museum.

Mary Timney was hanged in Dumfries for battering a

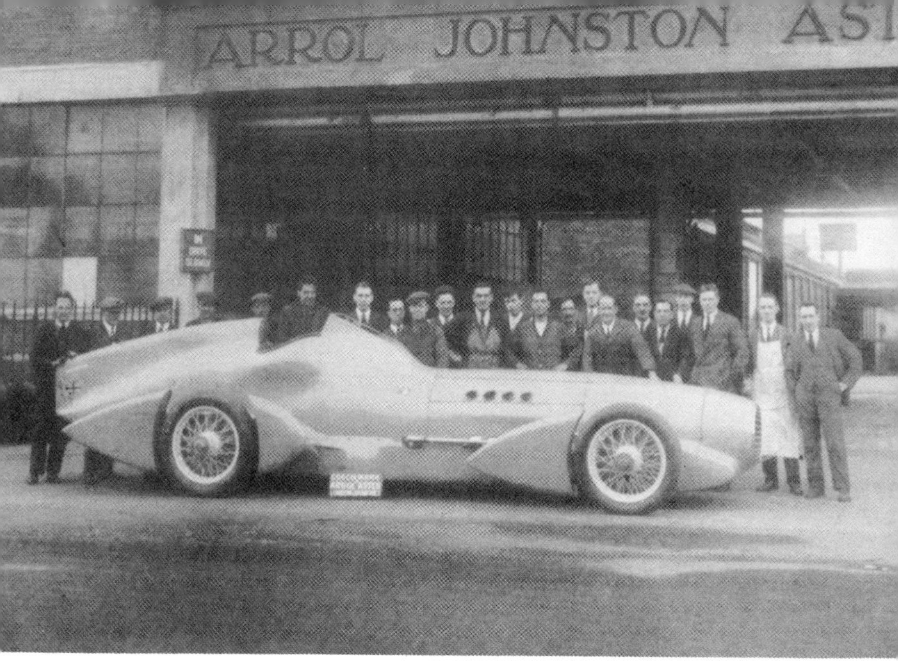

Malcolm Campbell's *Bluebird* built at the Arrol Johnston Car Factory at Neathhall, Dumfries. The premises are now occupied by Gates, makers of the famous 'green wellies' *(Courtesy: Ian A Rogers)*

neighbour to death with a mallet. Several national newspapers screamed for a pardon, because she was feeble-minded. But she was executed on a dull, overcast April day in 1862. Three thousand onlookers were controlled by fifty policemen, thirteen soldiers and 200 special constables. Prayers had been said for Mary in every church in Dumfries, and she literally had to be dragged to the gallows where the sinister Calcraft was waiting in his horrible velvet skullcap.

The murder weapon fell into the hands of a Penpont grain merchant, and his wife Elizabeth Grierson still possesses it. In 1988 English teacher Tom Pow wrote a play on Mary Timney which was broadcast by Radio Scotland.

Another 'last' for Dumfries was Scotland's last trial for witchcraft. The culprit, Elspeth Rule, was branded on the cheek with a hot iron and banished from the town for life in 1701. McDowall's *History of Dumfries* records that the barbarous sentence was carried out with such merciless effect that people living in 1790 had been told by their parents that the smoke caused by the torturing process was seen issuing out of the mouth of the unfortunate woman.

Dumfries had other eccentricities besides hanging people. Every May Day, the townspeople used to wear green and appointed characters as Robin Hood and Little John as 'lords of misrule'. They had absolute power in town for a day. In 1570 one Thom Trustre was fined for refusing to act as Robin for the day.

Another peculiar May Day feature was the riding of the 'Muckmen', or day labourers, out to Dalscairth wood armed with swords and dirks and wearing ribbons and sashes. When they reached the wood they each cut a branch of birch and headed out to the Stoop (now the site of an industrial estate). There they raced, and the victor won five merks and a silver 'muck bell' for the year.

The 'muckmen' had their own lord, and in 1688 the incumbent, John Maxwell, complained that his 'vassals' were not supporting him. He also complained to the council that he did not have enough money 'to drink their honours' good health'. Maxwell was granted half a crown, but was not allowed to fine the inhabitants of Dumfries. The May Day ceremony was scrapped in 1716 because of 'severall irregularities and misdemeanours, to the scandal of the place and dishonour of God'. By a majority decision the council prohibited the riding of the Muckmen, and ordered the treasurer to sell the bell to the highest bidder.

Dumfries has produced many famous people, among them Sir John Richardson, the Arctic explorer who was to count Darwin, Carlyle, Matthew Arnold, Wordsworth, Tennyson and Florence Nightingale among his acquaintances. He also had the pleasure of Burns's company every Sunday evening for three years. Richardson was six years old when the bard began teaching him the Scriptures in the family home in Nith Place. Burns was a bosom-friend of John's father, Gabriel, a brewer and future Provost of Dumfries, to whom he composed the following premature epitaph:

> Here brewer Gabriel's fire's extinct,
> And empty all his barrels;
> If as he brew'd he drinks,
> In upright, honest morals.

The poet's son Robert, and little John entered grammar

school on the same day, and Burns is said to have whispered to Gabriel: 'I wonder which of them will be the greatest man.'

Robert Junior became a clerk in the Stamp Office in London, but John became a renowned traveller, a ship's surgeon who spent ten freezing months holed up in Saskatchewan, the loneliness of which he described thus to his wife: 'The screams of a famished raven or the crash of a lofty pine rending through the intenseness of the forest are the only sounds that invade the solemn silence.

'When in my walks I have accidentally met one of my companions in this dreary solitude, his figure emerging from the shade has conveyed with irresistible force to my mind the idea of a being rising from the grave.'

Richardson was to make the first ever surveys of over 900 miles of the mysterious Arctic coast, and his drawings of the region's fauna were to impress Thomas Huxley the biologist. The Dumfries man's achievements in the medical field were equally formidable. With the 'Lady of the Lamp' – Florence Nightingale – he was an ardent hospital reformer and was the man behind the introduction of mild methods for treating lunatic sailors. He also introduced general anaesthetics to naval surgery and was the model for the doctor in *The Frozen Deep* by Wilkie Collins and Charles Dickens. He retired to the Lake District and is buried in Grasmere churchyard.

There have been moves to commemorate Richardson in street names in his home town – by none other than his brother's great-great granddaughter, Margaret Balmer, a mother of six from Dumfries. She has a lengthy pedigree, which includes the famous father of the American Navy, John Paul Jones, who was born in Kirkbean in Galloway. Another of her relatives was Sir James Anderson, whom she also wants to see honoured. Anderson, born in Dumfries in 1824, was the first man to lay transatlantic cables, thus linking the Old and New Worlds, in 1866.

Yet another of Mrs Balmer's relatives was a noted character: Chay Richardson, whom Alfie Truckell, the former curator of the Dumfries Burgh Museum, told me was the first in the area to build a 'river-bicycle' – on which he used to pedal up the Nith. When Chay, who was a local councillor, dropped dead, as a mark of respect no one would sit at his seat in the

Alfie Truckell outside Dumfries Museum with his successor as curator, David Lockwood *(Courtesy: Dumfriesshire Newspaper Group)*

chambers for a year.

Nobody in the Dumfries area can possibly know more about the town's past than Alfred Truckell MBE, who looked after the museum for thirty-five years. A well known archaeologist, he travels to Israel on digs and is a Fellow of the local Natural History and Antiquarian Society. A descendant of sea-captains, Alfie lives in the coastal village of Carsethorn along the so-called 'Scottish Riviera', which was once a hotbed for smugglers. (When he was young, Dumfries was an active coasting seaport, and there was a close maritime relationship with Liverpool. In fact, his tall uncle used to wear Merseyside policemen's trousers.)

Born in Barrow, young Alf moved to Dumfries as a toddler and was brought up along the Georgetown Road. Now a private housing estate pejoratively nicknamed Spam Valley on account of the trouble some residents have keeping up with their mortgage payments, Georgetown was then a quiet, rural village. 'Naked children played on the road, and there were rows of little home-made wooden bird-cages outside the houses, containing goldfinches and linnets,' recalls Alfie. 'Children from Georgetown came on barefoot the mile and a half or so to Noblehill school from April to October to save shoe leather. Most traffic was horse-drawn, although it is now the main Gretna to Stranraer road, and there are plenty of lorries.'

Alfie Truckell's Dumfries has become far less rural, although as recently as 1950, livestock was herded through the streets for market day. He remembers a bull bolting on the High Street, ending up in a first-floor room and falling through the ceiling into the shop below. Believe it or not, it was a china shop!

Alfie Truckell remembers the great police concerts, the operatic societies – and Harry Lauder and Charlie Chaplin heading bills at the Lyceum before it shut. He also talks about Stan Laurel at the Theatre Royal, Scotland's oldest theatre.

Alfie recalls the time Oswald Mosley visited the Loreburn Hall, when his Blackshirts clubbed hecklers senseless. He waxes lyrical about the four bridges which cross the Nith in Dumfries.

The Auld Brig, between the Whitesands and the Maxwelltown which Dumfries annexed in 1929, has seen much pageantry and history. A succession of kings and queens crossed it, last among them Mary, Queen of Scots in 1563 and James VI in 1617. Many a dragoon and redcoat has crossed the Auld Brig. A mob of Dumfriesians crossed it in the sixteenth century with torches in their hands to burn Kirkcudbright and massacre its residents. Boys scurried across the brig during the Jacobite Rebellion in 1715 to ferry beer, cheese and rolls to the Hebronites across the water. Robert Burns plodded over it many a time, and Alfie Truckell crossed it with 'twenty-odd Lebanese lads at full gallop in July 1981: they were waving their cedar-tree flag and singing the national anthem – the first time the bridge had seen that.'

The original Auld Brig, the traditional gateway to Galloway which began at the Brig en', had been built by Lady Devorgilla, John de Balliol's wife and the mother of the puppet Scots king, John Balliol. Before the lady built the bridge, monks and pilgrims forded the River Nith on their way to Whithorn.

There is still a steep street on the Maxwelltown bank called Pilgrims' Way (Maxwelltown used to be a village on its own before it was absorbed by Dumfries; and it was a notorious hideout for criminals. In fact, Sir John Fielding used to say that he could trace a rogue over the whole kingdom, but always lose him at the Bridge-end of Dumfries, or the Gorbals in Glasgow).

Pilgrims' Way leads to Observatory Hill, where Alfie Truckell's former stamping-ground stands. Dumfries Museum and Observatory was built on the site of a former windmill, which was put up in 1730 and ground corn for more than a century. It was run by the Astronomical Society until 1934 when Dumfries Burgh took it over. Nowadays Nithsdale District Council oversees the museum, which has many unusual exhibits including instruments of torture and execution and the signatures of James VI and Bonnie Prince Charlie. There is a fine collection of sculpted stone crosses and a spiral staircase whose central-beam is reputedly the mast of a vessel captured by Robert Burns during his days as a Customs officer.

The view from the upper floor of the museum is panoramic, and on top of the windmill is the Camera Obscura which gives a coloured moving picture of the town and many miles of the surrounding countryside (Big Brother is watching you – and has been since 1836 when it was installed).

The Old Bridge House, built into the Auld Brig, is another, interesting museum of Dumfries life.

Noel Dinwiddie is another man who will keep your mind occupied at numerous sittings. Noel is reverentially called 'the grand old man of Dumfries', and he is a mine of information on the town's past. He was eighty-six on Christmas Day 1988, and was still walking to his printing office on Great King Street, Dumfries, rain, hail or shine. He has been a long-time ambassador for the town he has loved ever since his clergyman father took him from his native parish of Ruthwell in 1910 to hear an announcement of the coronation of George V being read from the Midsteeple.

The 'Steeple' is the town's focal point during the annual Guid Nychburris celebrations and on Hogmanays when hundreds of Doonhamers (natives of Dumfries who live in far-flung places) gather there to bring in the 'bells'. The stationery firm Noel inherited from his uncle used to stand beneath the

Dumfries's coat-of-arms.

Steeple, whose clock now regularly chimes out *Scotland the Brave* and *Auld Lang Syne* thanks to the grand old man. He financed the installation of the mechanism responsible for the timepiece's new tunes, to mark the 800th anniversary of Dumfries in 1986. The songs are particularly appropriate in that Robert Burns lay in state within the Midsteeple before his funeral at St Michael's. Incidentally, the Midsteeple, which was opened in 1707 as a municipal centre, courthouse and prison, has a carving on it of the old Scots measure, an 'ell' (thirty-seven inches). And a table of distances shows the mileage to Huntingdon, where Scottish drovers drove their cattle during the eighteenth century.

An elder of St Michael's kirk, where Burns occupied a pew, Noel Dinwiddie was made honorary president of the Burns Federation in 1983. Nowadays he specialises in Burns napkins, which he prints and sends world-wide. He has also printed burgess tickets for a record number of Freedom ceremonies, including Neil Armstrong's, General Eisenhower's and Andy Stewart's.

Noel also recalls scrubbing piglets with a Norwegian major. Norway's link with Scotland goes back to the fourteenth century when Robert the Bruce signed a non-aggression pact with Haakon V – but it was cemented in 1940, when Norwegians, many of them whalers, fled Nazi domination to Scotland on whatever would float. They made Dumfries their home from home. The affinity between the Scandinavians and Dumfries folk was reflected in the similarity of their tongues. Newlands House, for instance, was requisitioned as a 'sik hus'.

Norges Hus, the HQ, was set up opposite the Burns Statue – where the trendy bar, Judy Chicago's stands today. It was a suitable coincidence that the Norwegians should plan a victorious return to their country a stone's throw from where Bruce began his fight for Scottish independence by murdering Comyn.

Thomas Watling was another product of Dumfries. Watling, who was a forger of £5 notes, was deported to Botany Bay and became the first artist vividly to portray Australia's wildlife. His rare talents were exploited by the Governor of the colony and the Surgeon-General. On his return to Scotland in 1803, Watling narrowly escaped conviction for getting up to his old tricks.

A Watling Street was opened in Dumfries in 1886, but it is not thought to be connected with the artist. In 1976 one of his paintings – the earliest one of Sydney in oils – was sold at Sotheby's for £31 000.

Since Watling had been one of the first 'Australians', he was particularly topical in 1988, the country's bicentennial year. And a special exhibition of his work at the British Museum was opened by the Queen. Nithsdale District Council ran their own a few months later in memory of the ex-convict.

Dumfries also has associations with the playwright and novelist, J M Barrie, who gave *Peter Pan* to the world. He received most of his secondary education at Dumfries Academy and was granted the Freedom of the town in 1924. At the Freedom ceremony he revealed that he had been inspired to write *Peter Pan* by 'a magical garden' next to the school and the River Nith.

Barrie has a street named after him, but when he lived in Dumfries it was at number six, Victoria Terrace – a fact recorded on a plaque outside.

Barrie was wont to say that he used to doff his cap to Thomas Carlyle, when the Sage visited his brother (Carlyle's) at what is now The Hill Hotel near Dumfries railway station.

CHAPTER 19

The Song-House of Scotland

When Robert Burns moved to Dumfries in November 1791, it was stated somewhere that even the most cursory observer would see his figure as that of an extraordinary individual. He was five feet ten inches, firmly built, symmetrical, and had a swarthy, intelligent face. A lot happened between then and 1796, the year of his death at his house in the Millhole, when he was compared to a plucked pigeon.

Allan Cunningham wrote of his return from the Brow Well on 18 July: 'The ascent to his house was steep, and the cart stopped at the foot of the Millhole Brae: when he alighted he shook much, and stood with difficulty; he seemed unable to stand upright. He stooped as if in pain, and walked tottering towards his own door: his looks were hollow and ghastly, and those who saw him then never expected to see him in life again.' He died three days later – and with his passing Dumfries became synonymous with one of the most celebrated men ever to have walked the face of the earth. Dumfries is recognised as the universe of Burns, and although his native Ayrshire claims him as its own, the Queen of the South has more places associated with him than any other quarter.

The bard had been granted the Freedom of Dumfries at the end of his Border Tour four years before he adopted it as his home. He began his final frantic and eventful five years lodged next to the Coach and Horses Inn, at number eleven, Bank Street – a street which was then called the Wee Vennel or the Stinking Vennel because of the open sewer which ran down the middle of the road on its way to the Nith. Thanks to the local historian Jimmy Urquhart, who died while I was researching this book, this house was saved the fate of conversion into public conveniences in 1969. He bought it, and even though he could not persuade the Scottish Secretary to finance its remodelling in the style of the late eighteenth century, it still stands as a monument to the poet. Outside hang two plaques, one of which – the work of Mr Urquhart – states: 'Here in the

Robert Burns, Bonnie Jean and family

Song-house of Scotland between November 1791 and May 1793 Robert Burns completed over sixty songs.'

Most of these songs were composed in a room no bigger than a bed closet. However, Burns and his large family soon shifted to bigger and better lodgings – a two-storeyed sandstone house in Mill Vennel (now the much-frequented Burns House) down the road from St Michael's church. He was promoted to the Dumfries Port Division as an exciseman but the war with France brought foreign imports to a standstill, and financial worries to Burns. His impecuniousness was, however, eased by presents of pheasants and game from the gentry and of barrels of oysters from some of his wealthy neighbours.

Burns died in the smaller of the two bedrooms at Millbrae, aged thirty-seven, his demise hastened by medical misdiagnosis. He had been advised by his doctor to go bathing in the Solway, but what was diagnosed as flying gout was really endocarditis or rheumatic heart disease.

His obituary in the *Gentlemen's Magazine* – read by many who today would fawn over him but who then would cross the street rather than meet him – stated that he had been a man 'who in his compositions has discovered the force of native honour, the warmth and tenderness of passion, the glowing touches of a descriptive pencil – a man who was the pupil of nature, the poet of inspiration, and who possessed in an extraordinary degree the powers and failings of genius. Of the former his works will remain a lasting monument; of the latter we are afraid that his conduct and fate afford but two melancholy proofs.'

The obituary writer of the local newspaper wrote, more sympathetically: 'His manly form and penetrating eye strikingly indicated extraordinary mental vigour. For originality of wit, rapidity of conception, and fluency of nervous phraseology, he was unrivalled. Animated by the fire of nature, he uttered sentiments which by their pathos melted the heart to tenderness, or expanded the mind by their sublimity. As a luminary emerging from behind a cloud, he arose at once into notice; and his works and his name can never die while living divine poesy shall agitate the chords of the human heart.'

The poet's politics had often got him into trouble in the town. Take for example his decision, as one of the founders of the town's library, to write an anti-Government slogan on the inside cover of a copy of De Lolme's *British Constitution* – and later donate it to the library. Regretting his action, he pasted the offending page to the frontispiece – sealing up his 'seditious secret' and greatly adding to the value of the book in the process. The book – its fly-leaf unstuck – is on display in the town's Robert Burns Centre. The suspect fly-leaf reads: 'Mr Burns presents this book to the library, and begs they will take it as a creed of British liberty till they find a better. – R.B.'

Burns was never reluctant to voice his support for the French Revolution. In fact he is said to have attempted to send some captured carronades, which were intercepted at Dover, to the French Convention. Louis XVI and Marie Antoinette were losing their heads; citizens of Dumfries were following the lead of the Provost and merrily burning an effigy of the freedom fighter Tom Paine. In the midst of this hysterical jingoism, Burns wrote to his correspondent Mrs Dunlop, that there was nothing to arrest a moment's attention in the execution of 'a perjured Blockhead (Louis) and an unprincipled Prostitute (his wife)'.

Burns saw the revolution as the struggle of ordinary men to

secure their rights. But, as his biographer Lockhart put it: 'He was the standing marvel of the place (Dumfries); his toasts, his jokes, his epigrams, his songs, were the daily food of conversation and scandal; and he, open and careless and thinking he did no great harm in saying and singing what many of his superiors had not the least objection to hear and applaud, soon began to be considered among the local admirers of the good old king and his ministers, as the most dangerous of all the apostles of sedition, and to be shunned accordingly.'

In October 1792, during a performance of *As You Like It* in the Theatre Royal, Dumfries, Burns was among a group who sang the *Ça Ira,* the song of the revolutionaries. Another account was that he sat in his seat during the singing of the National Anthem. He had some explaining to do to his employers, at any rate.

To commemorate the 200th anniversary of the French Revolution in 1989, Nithsdale District Council screened a series of French films and held an exhibition at the Robert Burns Centre. To mark the storming of the Bastille, councillors have suggested the planting of a tree of liberty, the reading of pro-revolution poems from the Midsteeple and a street fair with a French theme.

The Robert Burns Centre is the jewel in the council's crown. It was opened by Princess Alexandra in 1986, to mark Dumfries's Octocentenary, on the site of the Old Town Mill which had ground corn for 130 years and was later a hydro-electric power station. The centre doubles up as an audio-visual theatre and Burns exhibition area, and a film theatre: it earned three minutes' television on Film '87. There are several original letters and manuscripts at the centre, along with personal relics and a full-sized figure of Burns dressed in an exciseman's uniform. There is also a bookshop and restaurant called Jean Armour's Pantry. Audio-visual presentations are made regularly of 'Robert Burns – the Dumfries Years' and 'Dumfries – the Queen of the South'.

Burns's House is now also in the hands of the district council, and attracts its share of Burnsians from as far afield as Japan and Russia. The Globe Inn on the High Street also benefits from its description by Burns as his favourite tippling-house. It

Robert Burns Centre, Dumfries

has a homely little snug bar which has changed little since Burns's time, when he had an affair with the barmaid, Anne Park. The poet also scratched some verses on two small window-panes of the upstairs bedroom: lines from *Lovely Polly Stewart* and *Comin' thro' the Rye*.

The inn dates back to 1610. It is now owned by the Midland Bank Pension Fund, and is run by the grandson of a former President of the Burns Federation.

When Burns died, he was interred in a relatively simple grave in the north-eastern corner of St Michael's churchyard; and it was some time before even a stone was placed over his sod. It was not until 1813 that a plan was put in action to honour Scotland's national bard in a more suitable way. Sir Walter Scott, the Revd Henry Duncan and William Grierson played a prominent part in a world-wide appeal for funds to erect a mausoleum. Its foundation stone was laid with full masonic honours on 5 June 1815, King George III's birthday.

Over two years later, workmen opened Rabbie's grave in

Two locals of Burns's favourite pub *(Courtesy: Dumfriesshire Newspaper Group)*

order to move his remains to a new resting-place. According to the journalist John M'Diarmid, the poet was in a remarkable state of preservation – even down to the state of his raven-coloured hair and white teeth.

'The scene was so imposing that most of the workmen stood bare and uncovered, and at the same time felt their frames thrilling with some undefinable emotion as they gazed on the ashes of him whose fame was as wide as the world itself,' wrote M'Diarmid in his *Picture of Dumfries*.

'But the effect was momentary; for when they proceeded to insert a shell or case below the coffin, the head separated from the trunk and the whole body, with the exception of the bones, crumbled into dust.'

But Burns was not left to rest in peace. Scandalously, on the eve of Jean Armour's funeral in 1834, a phrenologist was allowed to take a plaster-cast of the poet's skull. As if they were witnessing an unveiling or something, some of the local big-wigs were permitted to tag along to get a glimpse of the deceased bard.

For the record, Burns's skull was twenty-two and a quarter inches in circumference. He received very high marks from the

Robert Burns's funeral, showing the funeral cortège entering St Michael's churchyard *(Etching: J Aikman, ARSA reproduced courtesy of Dumfries Museums)*

cranium-studier for philoprogenitiveness, adhesiveness, combativeness, love of approbation and benevolence. 'Uncertain' marks were scored for language. A Blackpool surgeon's report stated: 'Nothing could exceed the high state of preservation in which he found the bones of the cranium, or offer a fairer opportunity of supplying what has so long been desiderated by phrenologists – a correct model of our immortal poet's head.'

The next time dignitaries were allowed a keek at the bard's head was in May 1857 – sixty-one years after his death – when the vault was opened to bury Burns's eldest son. 'Little deterioration' was the ghouls' verdict.

The marble mausoleum of Burns – fashioned by the Italian Irishman Peter Turnerelli – is a grand monument of the Grecian style, although it was criticised for technical shortcomings. But that did not stop Turnerelli being granted the Freedom of Dumfries.

In 1936 the figure of the bard at the mausoleum was replaced by a more authentic one by a sculptor called Hermon

A ceremony at the Burns statue in Dumfries *(Courtesy: Dumfriesshire Newspaper Group)*

Cawthra. The original Turnerelli was consigned to a builders' yard, whence it has long since vanished without trace.

St Michael's churchyard is the final resting-place of other people of note, including Brother Walfrid, the founder of Glasgow Celtic FC. His grave is marked by a simple cross and a heart-shaped plaque. More than a hundred of his fellow Marist Brothers were buried in the churchyard. There is also an obelisk in memory of the 420 victims of the 1832 cholera epidemic.

To return to Burns: a statue to the poet was erected in 1882, cast out of marble in Italy. One writer criticised the work because the poet looked 'stolid, vacant and meaningless, certainly not the inspired, commanding look of Burns'.

He added: 'The base is crowded with inartistic paltry details – a bonnet, shepherd's pipe of an Italian type, mice, daisies and thistle, while the alleged collie defies description.'

The statue's original metal railings were removed for the war effort at the start of the Second World War. And the statue itself has been moved several times to allow for road improvements and other developments. In May 1958 all three tons, fifteen hundredweight of it was shifted from the High Street to Greyfriars' Church as part of the Castle Street Improvement Scheme. 'No piece of work has attracted so much interest in recent years, the reason doubtless being sentimental rather than technical', offered the *Dumfries Standard* of the day.

The 'stolid' Rabbie watched in 1989, however, as workmen sawed slabs below him as a prelude to pedestrianisation of the town centre.

Epilogue: 1989

Thirteen years after initial proposals by the International Burns Federation, Dumfries Burns Howff Club celebrated their centenary by paying over £700 to have Robert Burns's coat of arms matriculated with the Lord Lyon, King of Arms, in Edinburgh.

The arms depict a holly bush on a silver background surmounted by a club and a shepherd's horn. The crest depicts a woodlark perched on a bay-tree with the motto 'Better a Wee Bush than Nae Bield' ('Better a small bush than no shelter' is a rough translation). I am sure the stoic people of Dumfriesshire do live by that old Scots proverb.

Further Reading

Atkinson, Tom *South-West Scotland.* Luath, 1982

Blake, Brian *The Solway Firth.* Robert Hale, 1974

Blyth, Henry *Old Q, The Rake of Picadilly.* Weidenfeld and Nicolson, 1967

Bold, Alan *MacDiarmid.* John Murray, 1988

Brown, J. *The History of Sanquhar.* Dumfries, 1891

Crichton, D. *Sanquhar and the Crichtons.* Dumfries, 1907

Daiches, David *Robert Burns.* Spurbooks, 1981

Dinwiddie, Revd J L *The Ruthwell Cross.* Dumfries, 1927

Forman, Sheila *Moffat, A Backward Glance.* Lochar, 1987

Fraser, George MacDonald *The Steel Bonnets.* Collins Harvill, 1989

Gladstone, Sir Hugh *The Birds of Dumfriesshire.* London, 1910

Grieve, Michael and Aitken W R *Complete Poems of Hugh MacDiarmid.* Penguin, 1985

Hallewell, Richard *Walk South-West Scotland.* Bartholomew, 1989

Henderson, Thomas *Lockerbie.* Lockerbie, 1937

Kaplan, Fred *Thomas Carlyle.* Cambridge, 1983

Knowe, Cushie *Poems of Upper Nithsdale.* Holmes McDougall, undated

Lockwood, David *Dumfries's Story.* Farries, 1988

M'Diarmid, J *Sketches from Nature.* Dumfries, 1830 and *Picture of Dumfries.* Edinburgh, 1832

McDowall, William *History of Dumfries.* reprint Farries, Dumfries, 1986

McKay, James *Complete Works of Robert Burns.* Alloway, 1986 and *Burns – Lore of Dumfries and Galloway.* Alloway, 1988

McKenna, R W *Through Flood and Fire* and *Flower of the Heather.* Both reprinted by Farries, 1986

Porteous, Revd J M *God's Treasure-House in Scotland.* London, 1876

Ramage, C T *Drumlanrig Castle and the Douglases.* Dumfries, 1876

Rotberg, Robert *Joseph Thomson and the Exploration of Africa.* Chatto and Windus, 1971

Sinclair, Olga *Gretna Green, A Romantic History*. Unwin Hyman, 1989

The Statistical Accounts of Scotland. Dumfriesshire

Transactions of the Dumfries and Galloway Natural History and Antiquarian Society

Wood, J M *Smuggling in the Solway*. Dumfries, 1908

Wright, Robert *Dowding and the Battle of Britain*. Macdonald, 1969

Index